- CELEBRATING A -

Merry Catholic

Christmas

CELEBRATING A

Merry Catholic Christmas

A Guide to the Customs and Feast Days of Advent and Christmas

Fr. William Saunders

TAN Books
Charlotte, North Carolina

Cover and interior design by Caroline K. Green

Library of Congress Control Number: 2018909509

ISBN: 978-1-5051-1257-3
Published in the United States by
TAN Books
PO Box 410487
Charlotte, NC 28241
www.TANBooks.com

Printed in the United States of America

To
Bishop
William G. Curlin
(1927–2017),
friend and
mentor, who
loved Christmas

Contents

Introduction

I love Christmas. I have always loved Christmas. Since my ordination on May 12, 1984, I have looked forward to helping decorate the Church for Christmas and planning for the various religious festivities. As a pastor, I have always taken on the responsibility of setting up the manger scene and supervising the decorating in the church, which, for me, is not work but a spiritual exercise.

In an increasingly secularized society, I am saddened by the decline of the spiritual dimension of this beautiful celebration of our Lord's birth, even in Catholic families. Christmas seems to have become an economic period: Some stores are decorated in September and October. The business reports focus on "Black Friday" sales the day after Thanksgiving as an economic indicator of the future. Our homes are inundated with "holiday" catalogues offering their various wares. Then after Christmas, the business reports either rejoice or lament over the holiday spending period, and too many people suffer from overspending hangovers. Some academics have stopped using the traditional dating of BC (Before

Christ) and AD (*Anno Domini,* "in the years of the Lord") and have adopted BCE (Before the Common Era) and CE (Common Era); ironically, if asked, "What designates the BCE from the CE, one would have to say the birth of Jesus Christ—how foolish!

For some people, the focus is on the parties, the decorations, and the gifts. Greeting cards of mice dressed in Santa Claus suits, nature scenes, or even family pictures are sent without any mention of Christmas. Then the day after Christmas, empty boxes and stripped Christmas trees are placed by the curb ready for the trash truck.

And worst of all, the politically correct and secular ideology has pressured people to say "Happy Holidays" or "Seasons Greetings" or anything other than "Merry Christmas." Some government leaders even refuse to say, "Merry Christmas," and some refer to "holiday trees" and "holiday parties." Some localities even ban a nativity scene for being offensive.

In the pages to follow, I discuss some of the highlights of the "Christmas season." I try to show how many of our traditions offer the Catholic family rich opportunities to prepare for the coming of Jesus. In her wisdom, the Church helps us with our spiritual preparation by giving us the liturgical season of Advent. I discuss the beauty of Advent in general, and I look at a few of the great saints the Church honors during Advent. I also discuss the "O Antiphons," beautiful prayers traditionally prayed by the Church in the eight days (or Octave) leading up to the Nativity of our Lord.

The joys of a Catholic Christmas do not end with the birth of our Lord, of course. We have all heard of the "Twelve Days of Christmas," and I talk a bit about the true meaning of the carol. As you'll see, however, I also talk about the Catholic Christmas season—a period from the Nativity of the Christ Child up to the

Baptism of our Lord. We'll see that our joy expresses gratitude to the Holy Family: Mary, Joseph, and of course our Lord and Savior, Jesus Christ.

So the time has come to restore Christ to his rightful place of honor in our Christmas celebration and to make it a celebration not of *presents* but of his *presence*. I hope this book will help the reader to appreciate the beauty of Christmas and to recognize the great gift we have received and celebrate—our Lord Jesus Christ. The time has come for every Catholic and every Catholic family to celebrate a Merry Catholic Christmas!

Advent

What Is Advent?

For Catholics, the liturgical season of Advent motivates us to focus on the spiritual preparation for Christmas and the coming of our Lord. (Advent comes from the Latin *adventus*, meaning "coming.") The *Catechism of the Catholic Church* stresses the two-fold meaning of this "coming": "When the Church celebrates the liturgy of Advent each year, she makes present this ancient expectancy of the Messiah, for by sharing in the long preparation for the Savior's first coming, the faithful renew their ardent desire for his second coming" (524). Therefore, on one hand, the faithful reflect back on our Lord's first coming when he humbled himself, becoming incarnate and entering our time and space to free us from sin. On the other hand, we recall in the Creed that our Lord will come again to judge the living and the dead, and therefore, we must be ready to meet him to face our own particular judgment.

Advent also helps us to celebrate Christmas as though Christ truly is being born again. Christmas must not be celebrated simply as an historical event that punctuates our calendars, like many of our national holidays. Rather, Christmas must be celebrated as

a living event: yes, chronologically, Jesus was born on that first Christmas day (traditionally, *Anno Domini* 1). He entered this time and space.

However, in the spiritual sense of time, *kairotic* time, the saving action of the Lord Jesus lives beyond chronological time. His saving action is timeless. Therefore, Advent is a period for us to prepare for Christ to be born into our lives once again and to welcome him with a renewed faith, and to commit to living in his presence each day.

The Origins of Advent

The liturgical season of Advent marks the time of spiritual preparation by the faithful before Christmas. Advent begins on the Sunday closest to the feast of St. Andrew the Apostle (November 30). It spans four Sundays and four weeks of preparation, although the last week of Advent is usually truncated depending on when Christmas falls. (For instance, some years, the fourth Sunday of Advent is celebrated on Sunday morning—December 24—and then Christmas Eve is celebrated that same evening.)

The season of Advent has evolved in the spiritual life of the Church, and the historical origins of Advent are hard to determine precisely. In its earliest form, beginning in France, Advent was a period of preparation for the feast of the Epiphany, a day when converts were baptized; the Advent preparation was very similar to Lent with an emphasis on prayer and fasting which lasted three weeks, and then later was expanded to forty days. In the year 380, the local Council of Saragossa, Spain, established a three-week fast before Epiphany. Inspired by the Lenten regulations, the local Council of Macon, France, in 581 designated that from November

11 (the feast of St. Martin of Tours) until Christmas, fasting would be required on Monday, Wednesday, and Friday. Eventually, similar practices spread to England. In Rome, the Advent preparation did not appear until the sixth century and was viewed as a preparation for Christmas with less of a penitential bent.

The Church gradually formalized the celebration of Advent. The *Gelasian Sacramentary*, traditionally attributed to Pope St. Gelasius I (d. 496), was the first to provide Advent liturgies for five Sundays. Later, Pope St. Gregory I (d. 604) enhanced these liturgies, composing prayers, antiphons, readings, and responses. Pope St. Gregory VII (d. 1095) later reduced the number of Sundays in Advent to four. Finally, about the ninth century, the Church designated the first Sunday of Advent as the beginning of the Church year.

The Advent Wreath

In addition to being beautiful, the Advent wreath is a good, pious way to help us in our Advent preparation and part of our long-standing Catholic tradition. The actual origins of the wreath, however, are uncertain. There is evidence of pre-Christian Germanic peoples using wreaths with lit candles during the cold and dark December days as a sign of hope for the future warm and extended-sunlight days of spring. In Scandinavia during winter, lit candles were placed around a wheel, and prayers were offered to the god of light to turn "the wheel of the earth" back toward the sun and so lengthen the days and restore warmth. By the Middle Ages, after their evangelization by missionaries, Christians most likely adapted or "baptized" this tradition to produce the Advent wreath.

The symbolism of the wreath is beautiful and rich: The wreath is a circle, which has no beginning or end, so we call to mind how our lives, here and now, participate in the eternity of God's plan of salvation and how we hope to share eternal life in the kingdom of heaven. The wreath is made of fresh evergreen plant material because Christ came to give us new and everlasting life through his passion, death, and resurrection: Jesus said, "I came so that they might have life and have it more abundantly (Jn 10:10).

Even the various plant material used for the wreath has spiritual meaning: The laurel signifies victory over persecution and suffering; pine, holly, and yew, immortality; and cedar, strength and healing. The prickly leaves of holly remind us of the crown of thorns, and its red berries, the blood of our Lord. One English legend even tells of how the cross was made of holly.

Three candles are purple, symbolizing penance, preparation, and sacrifice; the rose candle which is lit on the Third Sunday of Advent, Gaudete Sunday (The Sunday of Rejoicing), calls us to rejoice because our preparation is now halfway finished. The light of the candles' flames represents Christ, who is "the Light that came into the world" to scatter the darkness of evil and sin and to radiate the truth and love of God (see Jn 3:19–21).

The progression of lighting candles over the four weeks shows our increasing readiness to meet our Lord so that by the fourth Sunday, when all four candles are lit, our hearts may be ablaze with love for the Lord and with anticipation for his coming.

Praying With the Advent Wreath

Each family ought to have an Advent wreath. Place it in the center of the dining table, light it at dinnertime, and say the special prayers (along with the normal blessing before meals). A traditional prayer service (passed down through the generations of my family) using the Advent wreath proceeds as follows:

On the First Sunday of Advent, the father of the family blesses the wreath, praying: "O God, by whose word all things are sanctified, pour forth Thy blessing upon this wreath, and grant that we who use it may prepare our hearts for the coming of Christ and

may receive from Thee abundant graces. Who livest and reignest forever. Amen." He then continues for each of the days of the first week of Advent, "O Lord, stir up Thy might, we beg Thee, and come, that by Thy protection we may deserve to be rescued from the threatening dangers of our sins and saved by Thy deliverance. Who livest and reignest forever. Amen." The youngest child then lights one purple candle; that is, the middle of the three purple candles.

On the Second Sunday of Advent, the father prays: "O Lord, stir up our hearts that we may prepare for Thy only begotten Son, that through His coming we may be made worthy to serve Thee with pure minds. Who livest and reignest forever. Amen." The oldest child then lights the purple candle from the first week plus the next purple candle.

On the Third Sunday of Advent, the father prays: "O Lord, we beg Thee, incline Thy ear to our prayers and enlighten the darkness of our minds by the grace of Thy visitation. Who livest and reignest forever. Amen." The mother then lights the two previously lit purple candles plus the rose candle.

Finally, on **the Fourth Sunday of Advent,** the father prays: "O Lord, stir up Thy power, we pray Thee, and come; and with great might help us, that with the help of Thy grace, Thy merciful forgiveness may hasten what our sins impede. Who livest and reignest forever. Amen." The father then lights all of the candles of the wreath.

Of course, this prayer service can be adapted to meet a family's particular needs (e.g., by allowing each child to have a turn in lighting the candles). One can imagine the excitement of a little child on seeing all the candles on the wreath lit, thereby showing that Christmas will soon be here.

This tradition will help each family to remain vigilant in their home and not lose sight of the true meaning of Christmas. In all, during Advent we strive to fulfill the opening prayer for the Mass of the First Sunday of Advent: "Grant your faithful, we pray, almighty God, the resolve to run forth to meet your Christ with righteous deeds at his coming, so that, gathered at his right hand, they may be worthy to possess the heavenly Kingdom" (*Roman Missal*).

Other Suggestions for a Good Advent Preparation

esides having an Advent wreath, here are some other suggestions for making a good Advent preparation.

First, Pray

Hopefully, prayer is already part of the daily routine, but if not, make it one. Pope St. John Paul II frequently said, "Families who pray together, stay together." Schedule a regular time for prayer. Also, pray the Rosary, individually or as a family. Ponder the various events in the life of our Lord, and the example of Mary, "the handmaid of the Lord," who gave of herself to receive the gift of our Savior. For little children, who have a shorter attention span, maybe just pray a decade each night, focusing on one mystery; over the four weeks of Advent, all the mysteries will have been prayed. Pope St. John Paul II also said that in praying the Rosary we gaze upon the face upon the face of Jesus, looking through the eyes of our Blessed Mother Mary.

Second, Read Sacred Scripture

Each liturgical year begins a new cycle whereby the Sunday Gospel passages will be taken primarily from either the Gospel of St. Matthew, St. Mark, or St. Luke. So, if a person reads one chapter a day, the whole Gospel could be read before Christmas (or at least shortly thereafter). However, do not just read the Gospel; rather, spend a few minutes reflecting upon it, inserting oneself into the passage, and allowing the Holy Spirit to speak in the quiet of one's heart.

The appropriate Gospel passages could be read during the praying of the Rosary. For little children, reading the stories from a children's version would be beneficial. In all, we are allowing the Word of God to penetrate and dwell in our hearts, remembering "the Word became flesh and made his dwelling among us, and we saw his glory, the glory as of the Father's only Son, full of grace and truth" (Jn 1:14).

Third, Take the Time for Confession

Do a thorough examination of conscience. If it has been a while since the last confession, find a good examination of conscience, and over the course of the week, pray for help from the Holy Spirit and write down those sins that come to mind. Bring that examination to confession, receive absolution, and do the prescribed penance.

Remember Psalm 51, which says that "a heart contrite and humbled, O God, you will not spurn." Remember that Jesus came to offer the perfect sacrifice for our sins and to reconcile us to the heavenly Father. Moreover, remember that Jesus himself instituted the sacrament of Penance to help us. On the night of Easter, the risen Lord appeared to the apostles and said, "Receive the Holy Spirit. Whose sins you forgive are forgiven them, and whose sins you retain are retained" (Jn 20:22–3).

Fourth, Teach

For children especially, read to them the stories of St. Francis and the first Christmas crèche, St. Boniface and the first Christmas tree, or St. Nicholas, who is Santa Claus. There are other good stories about the religious significance of Christmas greenery, poinsettias, and window candles. (These stories are found in this book.)

Fifth, Preach

To preach, one does not have to stand before a crowd or on the corner shouting Bible verses. There are subtle ways to preach the message of Christmas: Most of us send some kind of greeting card—use religious cards and religious stamps, and sign them with "May God bless you" or "I'll be praying for you at Christmas." When greeting people, say, "Merry Christmas," not, "Happy Holidays" or "Seasons Greetings"; people of goodwill will not be offended. Car bumper stickers or magnets depicting the nativity scene with the message to "Keep Christ in Christmas" are another easy way to evangelize.

Sixth, Preach By Actions

St. Paul warns us to be temperate and not overindulge. We do not want to act in a way unbecoming of a Christian, especially at a Christmas party; a Christmas party should not be a bacchanalia.

Seventh, Preach Also By Word

In conversation, the topics of religion and politics inevitably emerge. Some know-it-all will make derogatory comments about the Church, usually out of ignorance, and then pontificate about what needs to be changed. Defend the Faith, speak the truth clearly, and teach with love. We all know the "hot topics," so be prepared and be able to respond with clear, well-thought-out answers. The angels announced good news on Christmas, and we too must be the messengers of the Gospel today.

Finally, Give

Give of yourself by doing good works. Good works help heal the hurts caused by sin, including our own. You may remember the Advent calendars from Germany. A little door would be opened each day, showing a picture. These charming and instructive calendars were staples in Catholic homes in years gone by. You can still find them, but you can also make your own Advent calendar of good works. Start with a blank calendar. Each day do a good work—say a prayer for a person, help a neighbor in need, or make a sacrifice for a special intention. Whatever the good work, write it in the blank space. At the end of Advent, you will have a beautiful gift for the Lord.

For families with children, set up the crèche with all of the figures except Baby Jesus. Write the good work on a piece of paper and place it on the floor of the crèche or in Christ's crib. On Christmas, Jesus, Mary, and Joseph will have a home filled with our love.

Clean the closets of old clothes or toys and give them to a charity. Look to help an elderly person in the neighborhood who may be alone. For example, I know a family who on Christmas Eve buys blankets at the discount store, makes peanut butter and jelly sandwiches, and then takes them into the city to give to the homeless people they met. I know another family where each child uses his own money to buy a gift which is then given to a charity. In a world that can make us very self-centered and isolated, charitable works make us give of ourselves. St. Francis said, "It is in giving that we receive," and through our charitable works, we will receive the love of Christ himself.

So prepare this Advent to receive Christ as though he were coming for the first time. Make this Christmas a celebration of the birth of our Savior and the great gift of faith we have received. By striving to live in the presence of Christ during Advent, we will receive the best present of all: our Savior.

VIRGINI DEIPARAE
ET DIVO NICOLAO
GALEATIVS ROVELLIVS
AC DISCIPVLI D·D·
M·D·   XXXIX

Special Feast Days During Advent

St. Nicholas, the True Santa Claus (December 6)

St. Nicholas is one of our most popular saints, and the patron saint of Russia, Greece, and Sicily. Some sources estimate that over two thousand churches are named in his honor. Yet little historical evidence exists about this popular saint. Tradition holds that he was born in Patara in Lycia, a Roman province in Asia Minor (now Turkey), to a rather wealthy Christian family and benefitted from a solid Christian upbringing. Some say that, at age five, he began to study the teachings of the Church. He always strived to practice virtue and piety.

Nicholas's parents died when he was young and bequeathed to him a substantial inheritance, which he used for many good works. One popular story tells of a widower who had three daughters. He was going to sell them into prostitution since he could not afford to provide the necessary dowries for their marriages. St. Nicholas heard of the plight of the daughters and decided to help. In the dark of the night, he went to their home and tossed a bag of gold through an open window, thereby supplying the dowry money for the oldest daughter. The next two nights, he did the same. His generosity spared the girls from a sad fate. For this reason, he is the patron saint of pawnbrokers and brides.

His uncle, also named Nicholas, was bishop of Myra, Lycia, and he ordained his nephew to the priesthood. St. Nicholas then distributed all his wealth to the poor and entered a monastery, where he eventually became the abbot. St. Nicholas's reputation as a holy man spread. Upon the death of his uncle, St. Nicholas was chosen to succeed him as the bishop of Myra. St. Nicholas suffered imprisonment and torture for the Faith during the persecution waged by Emperor Diocletian around the year 300. After the legalization of Christianity, Emperor Constantine released him.

Later, he attended the Council of Nicaea (AD 325) and joined in the condemnation of the heresy of Arianism, which denied the divinity of Christ. During one of the council's sessions, St. Nicholas heard Arius deny the divinity of Jesus, and thereby his incarnation as true God and true man. St. Nicholas became enraged, approached Arius, and punched him in the face! The Council Fathers were appalled that a bishop would act this way and so stripped him of his episcopal regalia and imprisoned him. However, that night, St. Nicholas was visited by the Holy Family who restored his regalia and released him. When he entered the council the following morning, the other bishops were astonished and knew that this was a miraculous attestation to St. Nicholas's act of righteous anger.

Various stories have been handed on about this zealous and holy bishop: Once, he intervened to spare three innocent men sentenced to death by the corrupt governor Eustathius, whom St.

Nicholas confronted and moved to do penance. Another story is that sailors, caught in a ferocious storm, invoked his aid through prayer, and he miraculously appeared to them (although he was still on land) and helped them bail out their ship; hence, he is a patron saint of sailors. A final story relates how an evil butcher killed three boys and hid their bodies in a brine tub. St. Nicholas heard of this, confronted the butcher, and raised the boys back to life. Many other stories surround the life of St. Nicholas, too many to be recounted here. He died between the years AD 345 and AD 352 on December 6 and was buried at his cathedral.

St. Nicholas has been continually venerated as a great saint. In the sixth century, Emperor Justinian I built a church in honor of St. Nicholas at Constantinople, and St. John Chrysostom included his name in the liturgy. In the tenth century, an anonymous Greek author wrote, "The West as well as the East acclaims and glorifies him. Wherever there are people, in the country and the town, in the villages, in isles, in the furthest parts of the earth, his name is revered and churches are built in his honor. All Christians, young and old, men and women, boys and girls, reverence his memory and call upon his protection."

After the fanatical Seljuk Muslims invaded Asia Minor and

viciously persecuted Christianity, Italian merchants rescued St. Nicholas's body from desecration in AD 1087, and it was entombed in a new church in Bari, Italy. Pope Urban II, the great defender of the Faith and promoter of the crusades, blessed the new tomb with great ceremony. From that time, devotion to St. Nicholas increased throughout the West. During the Middle Ages, his tomb was the most visited by pilgrims in all of Europe. Interestingly, a liquid with the aroma of myrrh exudes from the tomb and wafts around; hence, he was soon recognized as the patron saint of perfumers.

ST. NICHOLAS'S ROLE IN OUR CHRISTMAS CELEBRATION

Traditionally, St. Nicholas has been associated with the giving of gifts at Christmas time due to the story about the widower and his three daughters. In Holland, where the custom seems to originate, St. Nicholas (or Sinterklaas or Santa Claus) comes on the eve of his feast day and brings presents to the good children. Another variant of this tradition is that, during the night, St. Nicholas fills the shoes of the children left near the front door with goodies, which they find the next morning.

Another tradition among the Germans is that, on the First Sunday of Advent, the children write a letter to the Christ Child in which they tell their secret wishes and the efforts they will make to prepare for Christmas. Then on St. Nicholas Day, he (or a reasonable facsimile) comes to ask each child about his progress, particularly about praying and being obedient to his parents. The good children receive apples, nuts, and other goodies, while the bad ones are chastised by Krampus, the small fellow who accompanies St. Nicholas. Krampus admonishes them, "You must change your lives, or else I will take you with me." The children, accordingly repentant, promise to do better and then receive their goodies from St. Nicholas. For this reason, many Dutch and German Christmas ornaments depict St. Nicholas dressed as a bishop with miter and crozier accompanied either by Krampus or a helpful angel who has the list of good children.

Sadly, the devotion to St. Nicholas was distorted by the Dutch Protestants, who wanted to erase his Catholic heritage. They stripped him of his bishop's regalia and made him a more Nordic looking *Father Christmas* with a red suit. They also interwove some of the legends surrounding the god Thor, who drove a chariot and who would come down the chimney to visit a home. In the nineteenth century, American authors also helped change the image of St. Nicholas as a bishop. In 1820, Washington Irving wrote a story of Santa Claus flying in a wagon to deliver presents to children. Three years later, Clement Moore wrote *A Visit from St. Nicholas* (known better as *The Night Before Christmas*), describing Santa Claus as a "jolly old elf" with a round belly, cheeks like roses, and a nose like a cherry. In 1882, Thomas Nast drew a picture of Santa Claus based on Moore's description and even added that the North Pole was his home; Nast was also well known for his anti-Catholic political cartoons. Finally, Haddon Sundblom, an advertising artist for Coca-Cola, transformed Santa Claus into the red-suited, rotund, and Coke-drinking jolly character we easily picture in our minds today.

WHAT TO SAY TO CHILDREN WHO ASK, "IS THERE A SANTA CLAUS?"

So what should we say to children? As a pastor, I would never say, "There is no Santa Claus," because there is—St. Nicholas. Saints live with our Lord in heaven, and they intercede for us. Granted, in our American society, little children may have a somewhat "blended" idea and grow up with the joyful thoughts of Santa in the red suit, in the sleigh with the reindeer, bringing the gifts on

Christmas. I remember believing in those things and going to visit Santa Claus at the department store. Those are joyful memories for me, and so long as parents keep the focus on Christ, they need not feel guilty about enjoying that magical time with their children. However, the time comes when a child begins to wonder, "Is there *really* a Santa Clause?" Or when the neighborhood kill-joy tells the child, "There is no Santa Claus."

Here, then, if you have not done so already, is the perfect opportunity to speak about St. Nicholas, the real Santa Claus, who inspires us to live the meaning of Christmas—to receive the gift of Jesus with joy and to share that gift generously. I remember reading once the response of the editor of *The New York Sun* in 1897 to an eight-year-old girl named Virginia who had asked, "Is there a Santa Claus?" Part of the answer, which still applies, was as follows:

> Yes, Virginia, there is a Santa Claus. He exists as certainly as love and generosity and devotion exist, and you know that they abound and give to your life its highest beauty and joy. Alas! How dreary would be the world if there were no Santa Claus! It would be as dreary as if there were no Virginias. There would be no childlike faith then, no poetry, no romance to make tolerable this existence. We should have no enjoyment, except in sense and sight. The external light with which childhood fills the world would be extinguished. . . . Nobody sees Santa Claus but that is no sign that there is no Santa Claus. The most real things in the world are those that neither children nor men can see. . . . Thank God! He lives, and he lives forever.

For me, this is a pretty good testimonial of St. Nicholas and the joy he brings to our Christmas celebration.

A SPIRITUAL OPPORTUNITY

Nevertheless, St. Nicholas reminds us that the greatest gift we celebrate each Christmas is the gift of our Savior himself, our Lord Jesus Christ, true God who also became true man. He came as the way, the truth, and the life. Through his cross and resurrection, he forgave our sins and gave us the promise of everlasting life. What a great gift!

Here is a great gift to be shared. First, St. Nicholas teaches us the importance of giving generously, especially to those in need. Honor St. Nicholas by performing a charitable act for someone else, especially a person in the neighborhood who is alone or elderly. Invite them to your home for a meal, or prepare a meal, or baked good and bring it to them.

The Solemnity of the Immaculate Conception (December 8)

Some people mistakenly think that the Immaculate Conception denotes Mary's conception of Christ by the power of the Holy Spirit. However, the Immaculate Conception is the belief that "the most Blessed Virgin Mary was, from the first moment of her conception, by a singular grace and privilege of almighty God and in view of the merits of Christ Jesus the Savior of the human race, preserved immune from all stain of original sin" (Pope Pius IX, *Ineffabilis Deus*).

It is interesting to notice that in our liturgical calendar, the Solemnity of the Annunciation on March 25 marks the time when Mary conceived our Lord by the power of the Holy Spirit. Nine months later, on December 25, we celebrate the Solemnity of Christmas, the birth of our Savior. Similarly, December 8 marks when Mary was conceived without original sin, and then September 8 celebrates her birth.

In the Gospel of St. Luke, we find the beautiful passage of the Annunciation, where Archangel Gabriel said to Mary (in our familiar wording as translated from St. Jerome's Latin *Vulgate* edition of the Bible), "Hail Mary, full of grace. The Lord is with you." While some Scripture scholars haggle over "how *full* is full," the testimony of St. Gabriel definitely indicates the exceptional holiness of the Blessed Mother. When one considers the role Mary was to play in the life of our Lord—whether his incarnation, his childhood, or his crucifixion—she must have been outstanding in holiness, truly "full of grace" in accepting and in fulfilling her role as the Mother of the Savior, in the fullest sense of *Mother*.

Going further to the original Greek text of the Gospel, we find the wording *chaire kecharitomene*. *Chaire* means "grace." The verb *kecharitomene* means "having been favored." The form of the verb is also important: here the verb does not simply imply

"fullness," but rather instrumentality. The late Scripture scholar
Father Carroll Stuhlmueller noted,

> Luke's word puts the emphasis upon the source of goodness rather
> than upon its effects. In regard to Mary, therefore, he points out
> that she is the object of God's grace and favor. . . . Mary is shown
> to have been chosen for a long time past; God's full flow of favor
> has already been concentrating upon her. . . . In her, more than in
> anyone else, God's messianic fulfillment is achieved. As such, she
> has received more from and through God's anticipation of Jesus's
> redemptive work than anyone else in the Old Testament or New
> Testament. (*The Jerome Biblical Commentary*)

Moreover, Archangel Gabriel announces, "The Lord is with
you." Such a proclamation coming from God himself implies a
particular office or a special prerogative. Again, Father Stuhlmueller noted, "The Redeemer-God professes to find an eminent fulfillment of His promises in the recipient of the greeting." Given
this scholarly examination of Scripture, we rightly believe, therefore, that an exceptional, grace-filled holiness extended to the very
beginning of Mary's life, her conception, and that God had prepared her to play an integral role in the plan of salvation.

Similarly, Archbishop Fulton Sheen thought that in his eternal
Wisdom, already knowing the plan of salvation, God dreamed of
Mary even before the world was made. Likewise, Vatican Council II taught, "The Father of mercies willed that the Incarnation
should be preceded by assent on the part of the predestined mother,
so that just as a woman had a share in bringing about death, so
also a woman should contribute to life" (*Lumen Gentium*, no.
56). Finally, the *Catechism* teaches, "'God sent forth his Son,' but
to prepare a body for him, he wanted the free cooperation of a

creature. For this, from all eternity, God chose for the mother of his Son a daughter of Israel" (488).

On the practical side, if original sin is inherited through our parents, and Jesus took on our human nature in all things except sin, then Mary had to be free of original sin.

Another beautiful dimension in understanding the importance and beauty of the Immaculate Conception is the role of Mary as "the New Eve" in the plan of salvation. St. Justin the Martyr (AD 100–165), in his *Dialogue with Trypho,* wrote,

> Jesus became Man by the Virgin so that the course which was taken by disobedience in the beginning through the agency of the serpent, might be also the very course by which it would be put down. For Eve, a virgin and undefiled, conceived the word of the serpent, and bore disobedience and death. But the Virgin Mary received faith and joy when the angel Gabriel announced to her the glad tidings that the Spirit of the Lord would come upon her and the power of the Most High would overshadow her, for which reason the Holy One being born of her is the Son of God. And she replied, "Be it done unto me according to thy word."

Unlike the Old (or First) Eve, who listened to the serpent (the fallen angel Satan), and chose to sin, thereby bringing suffering and death into this world, the New Eve, Mary, listened to the message of the Archangel Gabriel, and in her humility, became the mother of Jesus, who through his saving passion, death, and resurrection, conquered suffering, death, sin, and evil, and restored the life of grace. The Old Eve said no to God; the New Eve said yes. The Old Eve is the mother of all human beings who have inherited Original Sin; the New Eve is the mother of all the living, reborn by the grace of Baptism.

A FEW EXTRA INSIGHTS

The question then arises: how is Christ the Savior of Mary? Actually, much of the debate concerning the Immaculate Conception during the Middle Ages focused on this problem. Duns Scotus (d. 1308) posited one solution, saying, "Mary more than anyone else would have needed Christ as her Redeemer, since she would have contracted original sin . . . if the grace of the Mediator had not prevented this." Quoting the *Dogmatic Constitution on the Church* of the Second Vatican Council, the *Catechism* adds, "The 'splendor of an entirely unique holiness' by which Mary is 'enriched from the first instant of her conception' comes wholly from Christ: she is 'redeemed, in a more exalted fashion by reason of the merits of her Son'" (492). In essence, since Mary was chosen to share intimately in the life of Jesus from her conception, he was indeed her Savior from her conception.

Another question is: did the Church always believe in the Immaculate Conception even though it is not specifically mentioned in the Bible? One reason the discussion over the Immaculate Conception was prolonged is because the early Church was outlawed and under persecution until the year 313. After the legalization of Christianity, the Church had to address various problems surrounding the person of Jesus himself. More reflection about Mary and her role occurred after the Council of Ephesus (431) solemnly affirmed Mary's divine motherhood and gave her the title "Mother of God" in that she conceived by the power of the Holy Spirit and bore Jesus, who is second person of the Holy Trinity, consubstantial with the Father. Several of the early Church Fathers, including St. Ambrose (d. 397), St. Ephraem (d. 373), St. Andrew of Crete (d. 740), and St. John Damascene (d. 749), meditated on Mary's role as Mother, including her own grace-filled disposition, and wrote of her sinlessness. A feast day in honor of the Immaculate Conception has been celebrated in the Eastern part of the Church at least since the sixth century.

As time passed, further discussion arose about this belief. In 1849, Pius IX asked the bishops throughout the Church what they themselves, their clergy, and the people thought about this belief and whether they would want it defined solemnly. Of 603 bishops, 546 responded favorably without hesitation. Of those opposing, only 5 said the doctrine could not be solemnly defined, 24 did not know whether this was the opportune time, and 10 simply wanted a condemnation of any rejection of the doctrine. Pope Pius also recognized the spiritual malaise of the world where the rationalist school of philosophy had denied truth and anything of the super-natural, where revolutions were causing social upheaval, and the Industrial Revolution had threatened the dignity of the worker and family life. Therefore, Pope Pius wanted to recharge spiritually the faithful and saw no better way than presenting again the beautiful example of our Blessed Mother and her role in salvation history. On December 8, 1854, Pius IX solemnly defined the dogma of the Immaculate Conception in his bull *Ineffabilis Deus* (quoted in the opening paragraph of this section).

Finally, it is also interesting that in several apparitions of our Blessed Mother, she herself has attested to her Immaculate Conception: On December 9 (the date for the Solemnity of the Immaculate Conception in the Spanish Empire) in 1531 at Guadalupe, Mary said to Juan Diego, "I am the perfect and perpetual Virgin Mary, Mother of the true God, through whom everything lives." In 1830, Mary told St. Catherine Laboure to have the Miraculous Medal struck with the inscription, "O Mary, conceived free from sin, pray for us who have recourse to thee." Lastly, when she appeared to St. Bernadette at Lourdes in 1858, Mary said, "I am the Immaculate Conception."

In a homily on the Solemnity of the Immaculate Conception delivered in 1982, Pope John Paul II wrote,

> Blessed be God the Father of our Lord Jesus Christ, who filled you, Virgin of Nazareth, with every spiritual blessing in Christ. In Him, you were conceived Immaculate! Preselected to be His Mother, you were redeemed in Him and through Him more than any other human being! Preserved from the inheritance of original sin, you were conceived and came into the world in a state of sanctifying grace. Full of grace! We venerate this mystery of the faith in today's solemnity. Today, together with all the Church, we venerate the Redemption which was actuated in you. That most singular participation in the Redemption of the world and of man, was reserved only for you, solely for you. Hail O Mary, *Alma Redemptoris Mater*, dear Mother of the Redeemer.

As we continue our Advent preparation, may we invoke the prayers of our Blessed Mother, Mary Immaculate, to draw ever closer to our Lord, her Son, this Christmas.

A SPIRITUAL OPPORTUNITY

On the Solemnity of the Immaculate Conception, a family should gather for the Holy Rosary. Since it is Advent, the Joyful Mysteries most appropriately would be prayed: the Annunciation, the Visitation, the Nativity, the Presentation, and the Finding of the Child Jesus in the Temple. The actual Gospel passages could be read, all found in the first two chapters of the Gospel of St. Luke. Here would be a wonderful opportunity for the family to pray together and ponder the story of our Lord's birth and childhood, and the role our Blessed Mother played. We should never forget that Mary

is our Mother, given to all of us when he said from the cross to Mary, "Woman, behold your son," and to St. John, "Behold your Mother" (Jn 19:26–27).

Feast of Our Lady of Guadalupe (December 12)

December 12 marks the feast day of Our Lady of Guadalupe. The history behind Our Lady's feast involves St. Juan Diego, whose feast we celebrate on December 9. The story begins in the early morning hours of December 9, 1531, when a fifty-seven-year-old Indian peasant named Juan Diego was walking along the path of Tepeyac Hill on the outskirts of Mexico City. At this time, Mexico was very much mission territory, for Franciscan missionaries had only recently arrived not only to meet the spiritual needs of colonists but also to evangelize the native peoples. Juan Diego, like many of his family members, were among the earliest converts to the Faith.

Juan Diego had grown up under Aztec oppression. When Hernando Cortes arrived in Mexico in AD 1519, the native Nahuatl Indians (about ten million) were under the domination of the Aztecs. The religious practices of the Aztecs were extremely violent. Every major Aztec city had a temple pyramid, on top of which rested an altar. Upon this altar, Aztec priests would offer human sacrifice to their supreme god Huitzilopochtli, the sun god and god of war. It has been estimated that more than fifty thousand human beings were sacrificed each year to the Aztec gods. It is likely that the young Juan Diego himself witnessed an especially horrific event; at the dedication of a new temple to honor Huitzilopochtli, more than eighty thousand men were sacrificed in a period of just four days.

In AD 1520, shortly after his arrival, Hernando Cortes outlawed human sacrifice. Cortes, a Catholic, knew these practices were not only barbaric but also satanic. He knew that God had condemned Israel for its sinful acts of idolatry, including human sacrifice. In the words of the Psalmist, "They served their idols and were ensnared by them. They sacrificed to demons their own sons and daughters, Shedding innocent blood, the blood of their own sons and daughters, Whom they sacrificed to the idols of Canaan, desecrating the land with bloodshed" (Ps 106:36–38).

Cortes stripped the temple pyramid of its two idols, cleansed the stone of its blood, and erected a new altar. Cortes, his soldiers, and Father Olmedo then ascended the stairs with the Holy Cross and images of the Blessed Mother and St. Christopher. Upon this new altar, Father Olmedo offered the Sacrifice of the Mass. Upon what had been the place of evil pagan sacrifice, now the unbloody, eternal, and true sacrifice of our Lord was offered.

With this background, we can better appreciate the significance of the apparition of our Blessed Mother to Juan Diego as he walked along Tepeyac Hill to attend Mass on the morning of December 9, the date for the Solemnity of the Immaculate Conception throughout the Spanish Empire. On Tepeyac Hill, a pagan temple had stood to the pagan mother goddess Tonantzin, who was depicted in a most diabolical way as having a cluster of snake heads on her head and writhing serpents on her body. The Blessed Mother Mary would conquer and dispel Tonantzin.

Suddenly, Juan Diego heard beautiful strains of music. He saw a beautiful lady, who called his name, "Juanito, Juan Dieguito." He approached, and she said,

> Know for certain, least of my sons, that I am the perfect and perpetual Virgin Mary, Mother of Jesus, the true God, through whom everything lives, the Lord of all things near and far, the Master of Heaven and earth. It is my earnest wish that a temple be built here to my honor. Here I will demonstrate, I will

manifest, I will give all my love, my compassion, my help and my protection to the people. I am your merciful mother, the merciful mother of all of you who live united in this land, and of all mankind, of all those who love me, of those who cry to me, of those who seek me, and of those who have confidence in me. Here I will hear their weeping, their sorrow, and will remedy and alleviate all their multiple sufferings, necessities, and misfortunes.

She told Juan Diego to go tell Bishop Zumarraga of her desire for a church to be built at the site. Tradition holds that Juan Diego asked our Blessed Mother her name. She responded in his native language of Nahuatl, "*Tlecuatlecupe*," which means "the one who crushes the head of the serpent" (a clear reference to Genesis 3:15 and perhaps to the prominent symbol of the satanic Aztec religion). Tlecuatlecupe, when correctly pronounced, sounds remarkably similar to Guadalupe. Consequently, when Juan Diego told Bishop Zumarraga her name in his native tongue, he probably confused it with the familiar Spanish name Guadalupe, a city with a prominent Marian shrine.

Bishop Zumarraga was a saintly man. He was just and compassionate. He built the first hospital, library, and university in the Americas. He also was the Protector of the Indians, entrusted by Emperor Charles V to enforce his decree issued in August 1530, stating, "No person shall dare to make a single Indian a slave whether in war or in peace, whether by barter, by purchase, by trade, or on any other pretext or cause whatever." (Note that, in 1537, Pope Paul III condemned and forbade the enslavement of the Native American Indian.) Of course, some colonists ignored the decree and resented Bishop Zumarraga's protection of the Indians. At one point, the bishop was almost assassinated by those who wanted to exploit the Indians.

Bishop Zumarraga listened patiently to Juan Diego and said he would reflect on the matter, understandably doubting such a story. So Juan Diego went back to Tepeyac Hill and reported the bishop's response. Mary instructed him to try again. So the next day, he did. Although this time it was more difficult to see the bishop, Juan Diego prevailed, and the bishop once again listened patiently. However, the bishop asked him to bring back a sign from Mary to prove the story and her request. Again, Juan Diego reported the matter to our Blessed Mother, who told him to return to her the next day to receive the sign for the bishop.

On December 11, Juan Diego spent the day caring for his very sick uncle, Juan Bernardino. He asked Juan Diego to go and bring a priest who would hear his confession and administer the Last Rites. On December 12, Juan Diego set out again, but avoided Tepeyac Hill because he was ashamed that he had not returned the previous day as our Blessed Mother had directed. While making his detour, the Blessed Mother stopped him and said, "Hear and let it penetrate into your heart, my dear little son: Let nothing discourage you, nothing depress you. Let nothing alter your heart or your countenance. Also, do not fear any illness or vexation, anxiety or pain. Am I not here who am your mother? Are you not under my shadow and protection? Am I not your fountain of life? Are you not in the folds of my mantle, in the crossing of my arms? Is there anything else that you need?" Mary reassured Juan Diego that his uncle would not die; in fact, his health had been restored.

As for the sign for the bishop, Mary told Juan Diego to go to the top of the mountain and pick some flowers. He went up to the hill which was dry and barren—a place for cactus—and found roses like those grown in Castille, but foreign to Mexico. He gathered them in his tilma, a garment like a poncho. He brought them to Mary who arranged them and said to take them to the bishop.

Juan Diego proceeded again to Bishop Zumarraga's house. After waiting a while for an audience, he repeated the message to the bishop and opened his tilma to present the roses. The bishop saw not only the beautiful flowers fall from the tilma but also the beautiful image of our Lady of Guadalupe on it. Bishop Zumarraga wept at the sight of the image of the Blessed Mother and asked forgiveness for doubting. He took the tilma and laid it at the altar in his chapel. By Christmas of that year, an adobe structure was built atop Tepeyac Hill in honor of our Blessed Mother, Our Lady of Guadalupe, and it was dedicated on December 26, 1531, the feast of St. Stephen the Martyr.

The great fruit of the apparition was the conversion of the native peoples. Both the Spanish and the native Indians recognized that Mary was presenting to them Jesus, the true God, the Lord and Savior. Here is what they saw when they looked at the tilma: Our Blessed Mother's image surrounded by luminous light of the sun's rays, standing on the moon, and with stars on her mantle. Recall the description of Mary found in the book of Revelation: "A great sign appeared in the sky, a woman clothed with the sun, with the moon under her feet, and on her head a crown of twelve stars (Rv 12:1).

There are also symbols of divine victory over the satanic Aztec religion. Sunrays were symbolic of the Aztec sun god Huitzilo-pochtli. Therefore, our Blessed Mother, standing in front of the sun's rays, shows that she proclaims the true God who is greater than Huitzilopochtli and who eclipses his power.

She stands also on the moon. The moon god Tezcatlipoca was associated with hell and darkness, and brought evil, death, and destruction. Here again, the Blessed Mother's standing on the moon indicates divine triumph over evil.

Moreover, in Christian iconography, the crescent moon under our Lady's feet also symbolizes perpetual virginity and is connected with her Immaculate Conception and Assumption.

Her clothing also has special significance. The rose color of our Blessed Mother's dress has two interpretations, either as a symbol of the dawn of a new era or as sign of martyrdom for the Faith. For the Aztecs, pink and crimson were the colors of the earth.

On the dress are nine flowers which represent the tribes of the Aztec confederation. These flowers of four petals were known as the flower of the *quincunx*. For the Aztecs, this flower depicted the four movements of the sun (the four seasons) and the four directions (north, south, east, and west) united in the center which gives balance and equilibrium.

Her mantle is blue or turquoise, the color of the sky. This color represented both royalty and divinity, and was reserved for the emperor. The forty-six eight-pointed stars on her mantle indicate that she comes from heaven, as Queen and loving Mother. Interestingly, the research of Father Mario Sanches and Dr. Juan Hernandez Illescas of Mexico posits they are the same position as they would have appeared in the sky before dawn on the morning of December 12, 1531.

The gold brooch under her neck represents sanctity, and the bow around her waist is a sign of virginity. This bow, moreover, in Native Indian culture was the *nahui ollin*, a symbol of plentitude, fecundity, and new life. The high placement of the bow and the apparent swelling of the abdomen of the Blessed Mother suggest that Mary is pregnant. Just as Mary brought Jesus in her womb to visit St. Elizabeth and St. John the Baptist, so she did now to the native Indians.

The face of our Blessed Mother has the physiognomy of an Indian with its complexion, dark hair, and dark eyes. Her eyes are also cast downward, showing humility and compassion; whereas in Aztec iconography, a god looked straight ahead with wide-open, bugged-out eyes. Her hair is also straight, representing virginity; married women braided their hair. The image, therefore, shows that the Blessed Virgin Mary does not claim to be God, but only his messenger and loving mother.

Our Blessed Mother is supported by an angel, a symbol of royalty for the Indians. Some interpret this image as a sign of our Blessed Mother announcing a new age to come.

Given this recognition, the native Indians chanted, "The Virgin is one of us. Our pure Mother, Our Sovereign Lady, is one of us!" Within a decade, over nine million native Indians were converted to the Catholic faith.

SCIENTIFIC STUDIES

While the story of the apparition of our Blessed Mother at Guadalupe is a miracle in itself, Juan Diego's tilma is also miraculous. Since 1929, the Church has permitted various scientific studies to be performed on the tilma. The earliest studies detected images on the eyes of the Blessed Mother; namely, those of Juan Diego and two other persons (probably Bishop Zumarraga and Juan

Gonzalez, his interpreter). The images have a slight distortion, due to the natural curvature of the cornea and lens of the eye. Simply explained, because the eyes have moist surfaces due to tears, when a person is photographed, then an image of the photographer would be reflected in his eyes, and vice versa.

These findings have been repeatedly confirmed. Interestingly, Dr. Charles Wahlig, a nuclear physicist, posited that the Blessed Mother must have been invisibly present when Juan Diego was presenting the roses to Bishop Zumarraga and that the tilma acted like a photographic plate which captured her image and the reflection of their images in her eyes.

Infrared studies also revealed other unexplainable phenomena: The image was not painted, for the color does not penetrate the fibers as would paint. Weaving with such irregular fibers also produced a rough surface which would have distorted any simple surface painting, yet the image one sees is clear and undistorted.

Moreover, the tilma should have deteriorated long ago. It was not sized and has no protective coating. Anything of cactus fiber should have deteriorated within one hundred years, especially when exposed to pollution, candle soot, and the like. Nevertheless, the tilma remains unchanged.

Dr. Philip S. Callahan, a biophysicist, concluded:

The original figure including the rose robe, blue mantle, hands and face . . . is inexplicable. In terms of this infra-red study, there is no way to explain either the kind of color pigments utilized, nor the maintenance of color luminosity and brightness of pigments over the centuries. Furthermore, when consideration is given to the fact that there is no under-drawing, sizing, or over-varnish, and that the weave of the fabric is itself utilized to give the portrait depth, no explanation of the portrait is possible by infra-red

techniques. It is remarkable that in over four centuries there is no fading or cracking of the original figure on any portion of the ayate tilma, which being unsized, should have deteriorated centuries ago. (*Mary of the Americas*, p. 92)

The tilma has been a great source of devotion, especially for the Mexican people. However, the forces of evil have tried to prevail and destroy it, but have failed. For example, in 1921, during the fanatical reign of General Calles, who outlawed Catholicism, a bomb was planted in the basilica in hopes of destroying the tilma. The bomb reduced to rubble the marble altar below the tilma, shattered the windows, and twisted the heavy bronze altar cross.

Yet the tilma and even its glass covering were untouched. Just as Mary's apparition testified to the triumph of true religion over the bloodthirsty paganism of the Aztecs, even in this case, she overcame the forces of evil.

A MEDITATION

In sum, let us meditate on the beautiful prayer Pope St. John Paul II offered on January 27, 1979 at the Basilica of Our Lady of Guadalupe:

> O Mother, help us to be faithful stewards of the great mysteries of God. Help us to teach the truth proclaimed by your Son and to spread love, which is the chief commandment and the first fruit of the Holy Spirit. Help us to strengthen our brethren in faith, help us to awaken hope in eternal life. Help us to guard the great treasures stored in the souls of the People of God entrusted to us. . . .
>
> O Mother, awaken in the younger generation readiness for the exclusive service of God. Implore for us abundant local vocations to the priesthood and the consecrated life.
>
> O Mother, strengthen the faith of our brothers and sisters in the laity, so that in every field of social, professional, cultural, and political life they may act in accordance with the truth and the law brought by your Son to mankind, in order to lead everyone to eternal salvation and, at the same time, to make life on earth more human, more worthy of man.

The celebration of the feast of Our Lady of Guadalupe encourages us to be thankful for the gift of faith that we have received.

May we turn to our Blessed Mother, Our Lady of Guadalupe, to help us grow closer to the Lord, for she always wants to present Jesus to us and to draw us closer to him. May we also pray especially for those who have gone astray, left the Church, or entered a sinful lifestyle, that Mary will intercede with her maternal love and help them return to the love of our Savior.

St. Lucy (December 13)

According to tradition, St. Lucy was born to a noble family in Syracuse, Sicily around AD 283. Her father died when she was young, leaving her to the sole care of her mother Eutychia, whose name suggests a Greek lineage. As a young woman, St. Lucy desired to dedicate her life totally to the Lord by taking a vow of virginity and using her worldly goods to serve the poor. However, she was betrothed, albeit unwillingly, to a less than virtuous young man.

Because her mother suffered for years without relief from a hemorrhage, they visited the tomb of St. Agatha, who had been martyred a half-century earlier. Many miraculous cures had occurred there and had been attributed to St. Agatha's intercession. They arrived for Mass, and the Gospel passage for the day coincidentally recalled our Lord's cure for the woman with the hemorrhage. Lucy said to her mother, "If you believe what you have just heard, you should also believe that St. Agatha is always in the presence of him for whose name she suffered martyrdom; and if in this faith you touch the saint's tomb, you will instantly recover your health." After the Mass, they knelt before the tomb to pray.

St. Lucy fell asleep. St. Agatha appeared to her and said, "My sister Lucy, virgin consecrated to God, why do you ask me for something that you yourself can do for your mother? Indeed, your faith has already cured her." And indeed it had. St. Lucy then pleaded with her mother to allow her to remain a virgin and spend her dowry to help the poor. Her mother agreed.

Her betrothed, motivated by greed, was enraged. He denounced

St. Lucy to the Roman governor Paschasius. At this time, Emperor Diocletian waged a terrible and pervasive persecution of the Church. Paschasius ordered St. Lucy to offer the required pagan sacrifice to the gods and the emperor, which she refused. She answered, "The sacrifice that is pleasing to God is to visit the poor and help them in their need. And since I have nothing left to offer, I offer myself to the Lord." Paschasius replied, "Tell that story to fools like yourself, but I abide by the decrees of my masters." Lucy responded, "You obey your masters' laws, and I shall obey the laws of my God. You fear your masters, and I fear God. You are careful not to offend them, I take pains not to offend God. You want to please them, I wish to please Christ. Do then what you think will be of benefit to you, and I shall do what I think is good for me." He responded, "You have squandered your patrimony with seducers, and so you talk like a whore." Lucy continued her defense, and related Jesus's teaching, "When they bring you before synagogues, rulers, and authorities, do not worry about how to defend yourselves or what to say. The Holy Spirit will teach you at that moment all that should be said" (see Lk 12:11–12). This prompted Paschasius to ask, "So the Holy Spirit is in you?" Lucy replied, "Those who live chaste lives are the temples of the Holy Spirit."

For this, she was sentenced to a house of prostitution, where she would be violated. Filled with tremendous grace, she stood immovable, and the soldiers could not drag her away. They then piled sticks and brush around her, drenched them with pitch and resin, and ignited them; however, she remained unharmed. Her eyes were gouged out, but miraculously, she could still see. She then prophesied the death of Emperor Diocletian. Finally, she was slain by the sword. The faithful recovered her body and buried it.

St. Lucy has been revered since that time. She is mentioned in the Hieronymian Martyrology, the first official martyrology of the Church composed in the fifth century. St. Gregory included

her in the Canon of the Mass in his Missal, and her name is still mentioned in the Roman Canon of our present Missal. In the old Julian calendar, her feast day fell on the shortest day of the year (i.e., the winter solstice), and predictions were made for the next twelve months based on the events that occurred on the twelve days between her feast and Christmas.

ST. LUCY'S ROLE IN OUR CHRISTMAS CELEBRATION

Several countries have Christmas traditions surrounding St. Lucy's feast day. In Sweden, this day is called "Luciadagen." In a country where the sun does not set at all in June and darkness is around the clock in January, they rejoice at the coming increase of light with the winter solstice (again keeping in mind the dating of the old Julian calendar). On this day, the oldest daughter in the family wears a white dress with a red sash and stockings. She is crowned with an evergreen wreath with white candles. At dawn, she appears to the waiting family. They celebrate with hot coffee and lussekatter (saffron buns) or other pastries.

This celebration reminds us that Jesus is the true light who came into the world. The Gospel of St. John reads: "All things came to be through him, and without him nothing came to be. What came to be through him was life, and this life was the light of the human race; the light shines in the darkness and the darkness has not overcome it" (Jn 1:3–9).

A SPIRITUAL OPPORTUNITY

Therefore, as we meditate on St. Lucy during this Advent time, we remember Jesus is the light who came into the world to dispel sin and darkness. Like St. Lucy, we too are called to live in and radiate that light. Our Lord taught, "You are the light of the world" (Mt 5:14). Just as light itself is pure and beautiful, the holy life is pure and beautiful and gives glory to the Holy Trinity. Just as light travels in a straight line at constant speed, the holy life follows the straight path of truth with constancy, as revealed by our Lord, who is the way, the truth, and the life.

During our Advent preparation, we must strive to live in and radiate the light of Christ this Christmas through prayer and study to illuminate our minds to the presence of God, good works to radiate the goodness of God, and penance to purge our souls of sin and conquer weakness. May we be the beacons of light that draw others to Christ.

Yet we must be on guard. Another name derived from light, in Latin *lux*, is Lucifer, meaning "the light bearer," the once most beautiful angel who turned his eyes away from God and decided to gaze upon himself, who chose to follow his path according to his desires, and as such, fell from grace. During such a holy season as Advent, Satan attempts to take our eyes away from Christmas and seduce us to focus on the secular and material aspect, to dissipate our energies with many activities—albeit good—but in neglect of prayer and study; to prey on our weaknesses; and to provide the rationalizations to justify sin and the excuses to forgo confession. Yes, the devil wants to darken our eyes and keep us in the dark! Like St. Lucy, may we keep our eyes fixed on Christ, seek him wholeheartedly, and by his grace, come to a greater vision of him in this life, thereby allowing our Lord to say through our lives, "Let there be light!"

The Special Role of
St. Joseph, the Silent Knight

We must not forget the silent knight. Although St. Joseph does not have an official feast day during Advent, he is essential. Sadly, sometimes we do forget him. During Lectionary Cycle A, however, the Gospel passage for the Fourth Sunday of Advent is St. Matthew's recounting of the Annunciation to St. Joseph.

Nevertheless, he is often neglected as we celebrate Christmas. In much art work, including that depicted on Christmas Cards, St. Joseph looks like an old, bald man leaning on a cane and ready to fall into the crib with baby Jesus. Or worse, sometimes he is left out from the scene altogether. Once I received a Christmas card with a portion of a very famous painting of the Nativity. I saw baby Jesus, Blessed Mother Mary, and a shepherd; then there was an arm sticking out from the side that belonged to St. Joseph. Poor St. Joseph! I always make sure to send Christmas cards with a young St. Joseph.

What We Know of St. Joseph and Why He Is Essential in the Life of Our Lord

St. Joseph truly is the silent figure of the New Testament. For instance, the Gospel does not record one spoken verse for St. Joseph. Nevertheless, what this great saint did in his life for God speaks volumes. To appreciate him and his role in salvation, we need to glean the Gospels of St. Matthew and St. Luke.

St. Joseph was "of the house and family of David" (Lk 2:4). Because of his ancestry, St. Joseph is the link between the old covenant made with Abraham and Moses and the new, perfect, and everlasting covenant which will be made through the blood of Jesus. He brings to a close the notion of the Patriarch's promised land and King David's established kingdom, and prepares the way for Jesus the Messiah, who will establish the new kingdom of God and the new Promised Land—not a kingdom of land, castles, and armies, but a spiritual kingdom of truth and love, justice and peace. The kingdom of God established by Jesus is not confined to this physical world, but a spiritual one—a life shared with the Lord and lived now, and will be fulfilled in heaven.

St. Matthew says that St. Joseph was a "just" or "righteous" man. In other words, St. Joseph lived by God's standard, keeping the commandments and emulating God's love.

St. Joseph was selected to be the foster-father of our Lord. In the account of St. Matthew's, we read of how he was betrothed, or engaged, to Mary. Keep in mind that Jewish marriages—even for Orthodox Jews today—occurred in two distinct phases. The first phase was the betrothal, when the groom and bride exchanged vows. After this, they were considered legally married. However, they still did not yet live together; the woman continued to live with her parents.

The second phase usually occurred after a year. Here, the husband and a party of groomsmen would go to the home of his wife's family, where she and her bridesmaids would be waiting. He would bring her to his home to consummate the marriage, and they would live together as husband and wife for the rest of their lives. (This tradition is the basis for the parable of the five foolish bridesmaids in Matthew 25.) Keep in mind, therefore, that St. Joseph and Mary are married at the time of the Annunciation, even though both are virgins.

In the Gospel, St. Joseph learned Mary was with child. He must have been heartbroken, wondering both how this happened and what he was supposed to do. He knew Mary was most holy. However, he also knew the child was not his and that according to the Torah, the marriage contract was broken. In such a case, Mary could have been stoned to death in the public square for infidelity (see Dt 22). Instead of pursuing such a juridical act, he chose to divorce her quietly and let her go.

Nevertheless, the Angel of the Lord (presumably St. Gabriel) appeared to St. Joseph in a dream, revealed to him that Mary had conceived by the power of the Holy Spirit, and commanded that he take Mary as his wife and Jesus as his own Son. Without question or hesitation, St. Joseph did as the angel commanded. Pope Benedict XVI in his *Jesus of Nazareth: The Infancy Narratives* (pp. 41–42) provides a beautiful meditation on this scene:

> Once again this shows us an essential quality of the figure of Saint Joseph: his capacity to perceive the divine and his ability to discern. Only a man who is inwardly watchful for the divine, only someone with a real sensitivity for God and His ways, can receive God's message in this way. And an ability to discern was necessary in order to know whether it was simply a dream or whether God's messenger had truly appeared to him and addressed him.

The message conveyed to Joseph is overwhelming, and it demands extraordinarily courageous faith. Can it be that God has really spoken, that what Joseph was told in the dream was the truth—a truth so far surpassing anything he could have foreseen? Can it be that God has acted in this way toward a human creature? Can it be that God has now launched a new history with men? Matthew has already said that Joseph "inwardly considered" (*enthymethentos*) the right way to respond to Mary's pregnancy. So we can well imagine his inner struggle now to make sense of this breathtaking dream message: "Joseph, son of David, do not be afraid to take Mary your wife, for that which is conceived in her is of the Holy Spirit" (Matthew 1:20).

Here again, we see the important role of Joseph: he is to take Jesus as his own Son and to name him, thereby giving him legal recognition and legal personhood.

(Please note that the foregoing understanding of the Annunciation is the traditional one. Some individuals have speculated that St. Joseph knew that Mary had conceived by the power of the Holy Spirit and thereby felt unworthy, even afraid, to marry her and accept this responsibility; therefore, he decided to divorce her quietly. However, if he already knew what had happened, why then would the angel later tell St. Joseph in the dream that Mary had conceived by the power of the Holy Spirit? The traditional understanding is still the best one and is supported by Pope Benedict XVI.)

St. Joseph fulfilled his obligations with great fortitude. Throughout the Gospel, he faithfully and unquestioningly obeyed the commands of God: taking his family to the safety of Egypt to flee the wrath of King Herod; returning to Nazareth; presenting his child in the Temple for circumcision and formal presentation; and traveling to Jerusalem to celebrate Passover.

He accepted the responsibility of his vocation—being the faithful spouse of Mary and the foster-father of Jesus. He provided for his family as well as he could, whether that meant the stable in Bethlehem or the home in Nazareth. Although the Gospels recount hardly any information about the Holy Family's life in Nazareth, they were people of modest means. When St. Joseph and Mary presented Jesus at the Temple, they offered two turtledoves as a sacrifice, an exception made for poorer families who could not afford the usual offering of a lamb.

To provide for his family, St. Joseph worked as a carpenter. The original word in the Gospel is *tekton* which means "craftsman" or "artisan," thereby suggesting that he could well have been a builder of homes as well as a carpenter. As a good Jewish father, St. Joseph passed this trade onto his Son, and indeed Jesus is known as "the carpenter's son" (see Mt 13:55) and "the carpenter" (see Mk 6:3).

Although St. Joseph was not the physical father of Jesus, he was a *father* in every other sense of the word. At the time of the circumcision, eight days after the birth of our Lord, St. Joseph would have held baby Jesus in his arms as the rabbi performed the sacred ritual. When asked the child's name, St. Joseph would have replied, "His name is Jesus." Without St. Joseph, Jesus would have been a bastard child who had no standing in either Jewish or pagan Roman society. Also, as a good Jewish father, he was responsible for the religious education of his Son, including teaching him to read so that he could read the Sacred Scriptures.

Finally, Jesus must have loved and respected St. Joseph and Mary very much, for the Gospel reads, after the finding in the Temple, Jesus returned to Nazareth and "was obedient to them" (Lk 2:51). In all, St. Joseph selflessly set aside his own needs for the good of his family.

Moreover, St. Joseph must have been a fine, masculine example for Jesus considering that God, the Father, had entrusted his Son to his care. Archbishop Fulton Sheen, in his book *The World's First Love*, posited:

> Joseph was probably a young man, strong, virile, athletic, handsome, chaste, and disciplined, the kind of man one sees . . . working at a carpenter's bench. Instead of being a man incapable of loving, he must have been on fire with love. . . . Young girls in those days,

like Mary, took vows to love God uniquely, and so did young men, of whom Joseph was one so preeminent as to be called the "just." Instead then of being dried fruit to be served on the table of the King, he was rather a blossom filled with promise and power. He was not in the evening of life, but in its morning, bubbling over with energy, strength, and controlled passion." (pp. 77–78)

Tradition holds that St. Joseph died before Jesus began his public ministry. This belief is based on two points. First, he never appeared during the public ministry as did Mary, for example, at the wedding feast at Cana; and second, from the cross, Jesus entrusted the care of his mother to St. John the apostle, indicating she was a widow with no other children to care for her. Tradition also holds that he died in the presence of Jesus and Mary. For this reason, St. Joseph is the patron saint of a holy death. Although not defined by the Magisterium, St. Francis de Sales (d. 1622) believed that St. Joseph was assumed body and soul into heaven. He writes, "What is there left for us to say now if not that, in no way must we doubt that this glorious saint enjoys much credit in Heaven in the company of the One who favored him so much as to raise him there, body and soul; something which is all the more likely since we have no relic of him here below on earth. It seems to me no one can doubt this truth; for how could He have refused this grace to St. Joseph, he who had been obedient at all times in his entire life?" (complete *Works*).

The Testimony of Saints & Popes

Besides the aforementioned, other great saints have held great devotion to St. Joseph. St. Bernardine of Siena (d. 1444) preached, "He was chosen by the eternal Father as the trustworthy guardian and protector of His greatest treasures, namely, His divine Son and Mary, Joseph's wife. He carried out this vocation with complete fidelity until at last God called him, saying, 'Good and faithful servant, enter into the joy of your Lord.'"

St. Teresa of Avila (d. 1582) in her *Life* wrote, "I took St. Joseph as my advocate and protector, and recommended myself very earnestly to him. He came to my help in the most visible manner. This loving father of my soul, this beloved protector, hastened to pull me out of the state in which my body was languishing, just as he snatched me away from greater dangers of another nature which were jeopardizing my honor and my eternal salvation! For my happiness to be complete, he has always answered my prayers beyond what I had asked and hoped for. I do not remember even now that I have ever asked anything of him which he has failed to grant. I am astonished at the great favors which God has bestowed on me through this blessed saint, and at the perils from which he has freed me, both in body and in soul."

Popes through the ages of the Church have also recognized the importance of St. Joseph. Pope Pius IX declared him the Patron of the Catholic Church (1870). Pope Leo XIII in *Quamquam Pluries* (1889) wrote, "Joseph was the guardian, the administrator and the legitimate and natural defender of the divine household of which he was the head. It was thus natural and very worthy of St. Joseph that, as he supported in another era all the needs of the Family of Nazareth which he wrapped in his holy protection, he now covers with his heavenly patronage and defends the Church of Jesus Christ."

Pope John Paul II in *Redemptoris Custos* (1989) exhorted the faithful to look to St. Joseph in our troubled age:

> This patronage must be invoked, and it is always necessary for the Church, not only to defend it against dangers ceaselessly cropping up, but also and above all to support it in those fearful efforts

at evangelizing the world and spreading the new evangelization among nations where the Christian religion and life were formerly the most flourishing, but are now put to a difficult test. . . . May St. Joseph become for all a singular master in the service of the saving mission of Christ that is incumbent on each and every one of us in the Church: To spouses, to parents, to those who live by the work of their hands or by any other work, to persons called to the contemplative life as well as to those called to the apostolate.

Finally, St. Joseph has been honored in our liturgy. Since the legalization of Christianity in AD 313, a Mass has been offered in his honor, beginning in the East. Pope John XXIII in 1962 ordered St. Joseph's name inserted into the Roman Canon (Eucharistic Prayer I), as did Pope Francis in 2013 for the other Eucharistic Prayers, a proper recognition for the Guardian of the Universal Church. Moreover, St. Joseph's feast day of March 19 is a solemnity and traditionally a holy day of obligation throughout the universal Church (*Code of Canon Law*, no. 1246). In 1955, Pope Pius XII established the Feast of St. Joseph the Worker on May 1 to present St. Joseph as the exemplar of all working people and to focus on the true dignity of human labor in contrast to the "May Day" celebrations of communist countries.

A Spiritual Opportunity

A beautiful activity to honor St. Joseph during Advent would be to establish your own "St. Joseph Day." This would be some day before Christmas when the family goes together to buy or cut down the Christmas tree. (It may also be the day when the family unpacks and erects the artificial tree.) I would suggest doing so on the Third or Fourth Sunday of Advent.

The family could then decorate the tree together with the father placing the first ornament at the top of the tree—maybe a star or an angel. When the tree is decorated, and its lights turned on, the father could then read to the family the story of St. Boniface and the first Christmas tree, or St. Francis and the first crèche (stories found in this book). A joyful singing of *Silent Night* could then follow, with all the room lights turned off. Finally, a merry enjoyment of hot chocolate and cookies would be appropriate with a toast to good St. Joseph.

A St. Joseph Christmas Story

In 1850, Bishop Jean Baptiste Lamy was appointed as the bishop of the New Mexico Territory, with the cathedral located at the city of Santa Fe. Bishop Lamy said, "I have 6,000 Catholics and 300 Americans." To meet the spiritual needs of this vast territory, he pleaded to various religious communities.

In 1852, the Sisters of Loretto responded and sent seven sisters to Santa Fe to establish a school, the Academy of Our Lady of Light (Loretto), which opened the following year. As the years went by and the school prospered, the Sisters desired to build a beautiful chapel. Bishop Lamy encouraged the Sisters to use the architectural services of Antoine Mouly from Paris, France, who was also in charge of building the cathedral. Since Mouly had been involved in the renovation and restoration of Sainte Chapelle in Paris, he designed the Sisters' chapel in a similar French Gothic style. Work began in July 1873. Mother Magdalen wrote in her diary that the construction was entrusted to St. Joseph, "in whose honor we communicated every Wednesday, that he might assist us. Of his powerful help, we have been witnesses on several occasions."

The construction was completed in 1878. However, there was

one problem: there was no way to access the choir loft, which was located twenty-two feet above the ground floor. So Mother Magdalen interviewed various carpenters, but none seemed to have a solution. Most recommended using a ladder since a staircase would require too much floor space.

Not losing hope, the Sisters began a novena to St. Joseph, the patron saint of carpenters. On the ninth day of the novena, a gray-haired man arrived at the convent with his donkey and his toolbox. He asked Mother Magdalen if he might try to build a staircase and solve the Sisters' problem.

He worked for three months by himself. His only tools were a saw, a hammer, a T-square, and a few tubs of water for soaking the wood to make it pliable. The carpenter finished his job, right in time for Christmas Midnight Mass. When the Sisters went to thank him and pay him for his work, he had disappeared. The Sisters even placed advertisements in local papers to contact the carpenter or find information about him, but nothing ever arose. Mother Magdalen and the Sisters were convinced that St. Joseph himself, the quiet carpenter, had answered their prayers and fulfilled their need.

The staircase since then has been known as "the miraculous staircase." It has two 360 degree turns and no central support beam (or newel)—it is free standing. No nails were used, only square wooden pegs. The stairs are perfectly curved. The risers of the thirty-three steps are all the same height. (A coincidence—thirty-three steps for thirty-three years of our Lord's life?) Experts have tried to identify the wood, but it remains a mystery, only called "an edge-grained fir of some sort," which is not available in New Mexico and some suggest even extinct. Engineers have stated that the staircase defies the laws of gravity and should have collapsed. Only ten years after the construction was a balustrade added. Thank you, St. Joseph.

The Octave Before Christmas

The Octave before Christmas is a special period of our Advent preparation. This time is especially highlighted in praying Vespers of the Liturgy of the Hours. From December 17 to December 23, the O Antiphons accompany the recitation of the Canticle of Mary, also known as the Magnificat (see Lk 1:46–55). (An antiphon is a verse which precedes the recitation of the psalms or canticles.) These "O" Antiphons highlight titles of our Lord, who is to be born on Christmas Day. They also serve as the basis for the Advent hymn *O Come, O Come Emmanuel*.

The importance of the O Antiphons is twofold: Each one highlights a title for the Messiah: *O Sapientia* (O Wisdom), *O Adonai* (O Lord), *O Radix Jesse* (O Root of Jesse), *O Clavis David* (O Key of David), *O Oriens* (O Rising Sun), *O Rex Gentium* (O King of the Nations), and *O Emmanuel* (God is with us). Also, each antiphon refers to the prophecy of Isaiah of the coming of the Messiah. By meditating on each title and the prophecy, one can better appreciate who Jesus is and how his role as Savior fulfills God's promises.

The exact origin of the O Antiphons is not known. Boethius (c. 480–524) made a slight reference to them, thereby suggesting their presence at that time. At the Benedictine Abbey of Fleury (now Saint-Benoit-sur-Loire), these antiphons were recited by the abbot and other abbey leaders in descending rank, and then a gift was given to each member of the community. By the eighth century, they were in use in the liturgical celebrations in Rome. The usage of the O Antiphons was so prevalent in monasteries that the phrases "keep your O" and "the Great O Antiphons" were common parlance. One may thereby conclude that in some fashion the O Antiphons have been part of our liturgical tradition since the very early Church.

Let's look at each antiphon with just a sample of Isaiah's related prophecies and their fulfillment in Christ:

O Sapientia

"O Wisdom, O holy Word of God, you govern all creation with your strong yet tender care. Come and show your people the way to salvation."

Isaiah had prophesied that "the spirit of the Lord shall rest upon him: a spirit of wisdom and of understanding, A spirit of counsel and of strength, a spirit of knowledge and of fear of the Lord, and his delight shall be the fear of the Lord" (Is 11:2–3); and "wonderful is his counsel and great his wisdom" (Is 28:29). In the Gospel of St. Luke, we read after the finding in the Temple, "Jesus advanced [in] wisdom and age and favor before God and man" (Lk 2:52); and at the beginning of the public ministry, Jesus quoted Isaiah, saying that "the Spirit of the Lord is upon me" (Lk 4:18–9).

O Adonai

"O sacred Lord of ancient Israel, who showed yourself to Moses in the burning bush, who gave him the holy law on Sinai mountain: come, stretch out your mighty hand to set us free."

Isaiah had prophesied, "But he shall judge the poor with justice, and decide aright for the land's afflicted. He shall strike the ruthless with the rod of his mouth, and with the breath of his lips he shall slay the wicked. Justice shall be the band around his waist, and faithfulness a belt upon his hips" (Is 11:4–5); and, "Indeed the Lord will be there with us, majestic; yes, the Lord our judge, the Lord our lawgiver, the Lord our king, he it is who will save us" (Is 33:22). Throughout the Gospels, Jesus is recognized as "Lord" by both Jew and Gentile.

O Radix Jesse

"O Flower of Jesse's stem, you have been raised up as a sign for all peoples; kings stand silent in your presence; the nations bow down in worship before you. Come, let nothing keep you from coming to our aid."

Isaiah had prophesied, "A shoot shall sprout from the stump of Jesse, and from his roots a bud shall blossom" (Is 11:1); and, "On that day, the root of Jesse, set up as a signal for the nations, the Gentiles shall seek out, for his dwelling shall be glorious" (Is 11:10). Remember also that Jesse was the father of King David, and the prophet Micah had prophesied that the Messiah would be of the house and lineage of David and be born in David's city, Bethlehem (Mi 5:1), which the Gospel of St. Matthew quotes (Mt 2:6). St. Matthew also emphasizes that St. Joseph is of the lineage of King David, and hence Jesse (Mt 1:1–16, 20). In the book of Revelation, Jesus announces, "I am the Root and Offspring of David" (Rv 22:16).

O Clavis David

"O Key of David, O royal Power of Israel controlling at your will the gate of Heaven: Come, break down the prison walls of death for those who dwell in darkness and the shadow of death; and lead your captive people into freedom."

Isaiah had prophesied, "I will place the Key of the House of David on his shoulder; when he opens, no one will shut, when he shuts, no one will open" (Is 22:22), and, "His dominion is vast and forever peaceful, from David's throne, and over his kingdom, which he confirms and sustains by judgment and justice, both now and forever" (Is 9:6). In the Gospel of St. Matthew, Jesus entrusts the "keys of heaven" to St. Peter, signifying that after his authority will be Peter's as pope (Mt 16:19), and in the book of Revelation, Jesus announces, "I hold the keys of death and the netherworld" (Rv 91:18).

O Oriens

"O Radiant Dawn, splendor of eternal light, sun of justice: come, shine on those who dwell in darkness and the shadow of death."

Isaiah had prophesied, "The people who walked in darkness have seen a great light; upon those who dwelt in the land of gloom a light has shown" (Is 9:1). In the book of Revelation, Jesus announces, "I am the Morning Star shining bright" (Rv 22:16). Remember that a star rose in the East, proclaiming the birth of the Messiah (Mt 2:1ff.), and that the priest Simeon, at the time of the Presentation, proclaimed, "Now, Master, you can dismiss your servant in peace; you have fulfilled your word. For my eyes have witnessed your saving deed displayed for all the peoples to see: A revealing light to the Gentiles, the glory of your people Israel" (Lk 2:29–32).

O Rex Gentium

"O King of all the nations, the only joy of every human heart; O Keystone of the mighty arch of man, come and save the creature you fashioned from the dust."

Isaiah had prophesied, "For a child is born to us, a son is given us; upon his shoulder dominion rests. They name him Wonder-Counselor, God-Hero, Father-Forever, Prince of Peace" (Is 9:5), and, "He shall judge between the nations, and impose terms on many peoples. They shall beat their swords into plowshares and their spears into pruning hooks; one nation shall not raise the sword against another, nor shall they train for war again" (Is 2:4). Here again resounds the proclamation of the priest Simeon at the time of the Presentation, that Jesus is the Messiah who came to gather all peoples, Jew and Gentile.

O Emmanuel

"O Emmanuel, king and lawgiver, desire of the nations, Savior of all people, come and set us free, Lord our God."

Isaiah had prophesied, "The Lord himself will give you this sign: the Virgin shall be with child, and bear a son, and shall name him Emmanuel" (Is 7:14). Remember *emmanuel* means "God is with us." The Gospel of St. Matthew quotes this very verse, during the annunciation to St. Joseph by the angel (Mt 1:23).

According to Professor Robert Greenberg of the San Francisco Conservatory of Music, the Benedictine monks arranged these antiphons with a definite purpose. If one starts with the last title and takes the first letter of each one—Emmanuel, **Rex, Oriens, Clavis, Radix, Adonai, Sapientia**—the Latin words *ero cras* are formed, meaning, "tomorrow, I will come." Therefore, the Lord Jesus, whose coming we have prepared for in Advent and whom we have addressed in these seven Messianic titles, now speaks to us, "Tomorrow, I will come." So the O Antiphons not only bring intensity to our Advent preparation but also bring it to a joyful conclusion.

A Spiritual Opportunity

The Council of Vatican II taught that "the Divine Office is the voice of the church, that is, of the whole mystical body publicly

praising God" (*Sacrosanctum Concilium*, no. 99). The praying of the Divine Office is not only for priests and religious; the laity are also encouraged to pray the Office.

Here is an opportunity to suggest to the pastor of the parish to offer a celebration of Vespers during the Octave. If such a celebration is not feasible, the laity may still pray Vespers individually or as a family. The Divine Office is even available through internet resources. Here is a good opportunity not only to learn more about the Divine Office but also to begin a daily practice of praying at least part of it in union with the whole Church.

Another family activity would be to sing the appropriate verse of the hymn O *Come, O Come, Emmanuel* each evening during the Octave, maybe at dinner after the lighting of the Advent Wreath. We can see the O Antiphons in this favorite hymn if we look. The verses are as follows:

> O come, O come, **Emmanuel,**
> And ransom captive Israel,
> That mourns in lonely exile here
> Until the Son of God appear.
>
> *Chorus*
> Rejoice! Rejoice! Emmanuel.
> Shall come to thee, O Israel.
>
> O come, thou, **Wisdom** from on high,
> Who ord'rest all things mightily;
> To us the path of knowledge show,
> And teach us in her ways to go. *Chorus*

O come, O come, thou **Lord** of might,
Who to thy tribes on Sinai's height
In ancient times didst give the law,
In cloud, and majesty, and awe. *Chorus*

O come, thou **Branch** of Jesse's tree,
Free them from Satan's tyranny
That trust thy mighty pow'r to save,
And give them vict'ry o'er the grave. *Chorus*

O come, thou **Key** of David, come,
And open wide our heav'nly home;
Make safe the way that leads on high,
And close the path to misery. *Chorus*

O come, thou **Dayspring** from on high,
And cheer us by thy drawing nigh
Disperse the gloomy clouds of night,
And death's dark shadow put to flight. *Chorus*

O come, Desire of nations, bind
In one the hearts of all mankind;
Bid though our sad divisions cease,
And by thyself our **King** of peace. *Chorus*

To keep the sequence of the O Antiphons, one would have to move the first verse to last place. Either way, this hymn provides a beautiful catechesis for preparation for Christmas.

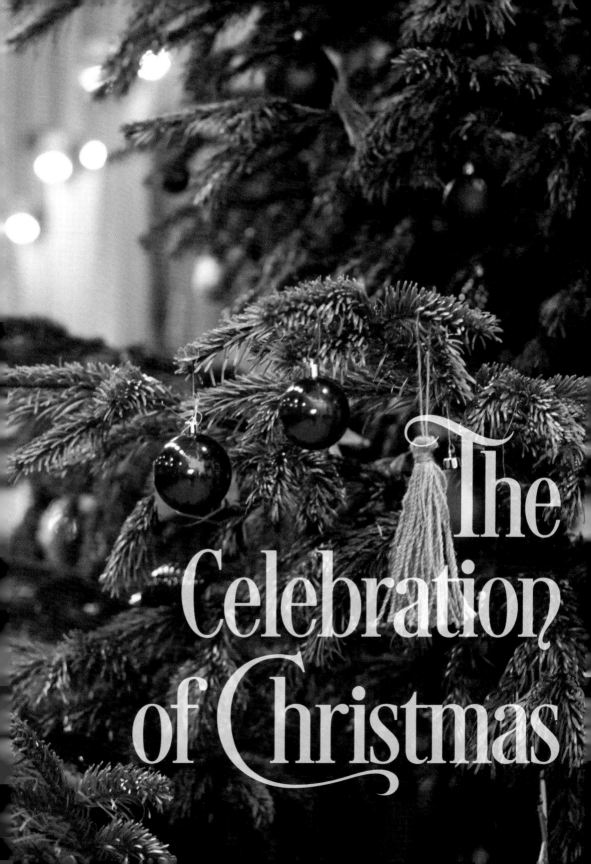

The
Celebration
of Christmas

The Twelve Days of Christmas

The carol "The Twelve Days of Christmas" marks the time span between Christmas, December 25, and Epiphany, January 6. While the song is rather whimsical (if not annoyingly repetitive), it has a great catechetical value. A little background history is important for understanding the significance of the carol.

Beginning with the reign of Queen Elizabeth I of England in 1558, the Roman Catholic Church and any practice of the Faith were strictly forbidden. The Mass was outlawed. Priests were expelled from the realm and threatened with the charge of high treason, with the punishment of being hanged, drawn, and quartered for returning and offering Mass. Any Catholic harboring a priest in the home or allowing him to offer Mass was subject to the same penalty. Catholic citizens were not allowed to vote, to hold property, to be witnesses in court, or to have weapons. Anyone who did not attend Protestant services was fined and imprisoned for repeated offenses. All Catholic schools were closed and instruction in the Faith was forbidden. Anyone appointed to a civil office had to take an oath denouncing the pope and the belief in transubstantiation, thereby, in effect, preventing any Catholic from such positions. These laws remained in effect until April 1829 when King George IV reluctantly signed the Emancipation Bill granting political and religious freedom to Catholics. However, to this day, the king or queen of the United Kingdom cannot be a Roman Catholic.

Please note that these same penal laws were enforced in the Thirteen Colonies until the time of the Revolutionary War. Also, the intensity of enforcement of these laws depended upon the particular reign. For example, during the time of the Commonwealth under Oliver Cromwell (1642–1660), the Puritan Parliament even outlawed the celebration of Christmas.

The song "The Twelve Days of Christmas" was written in England sometime in the mid-1700s using seemingly secular images or symbols to help catechize children in the Faith. The **"true love"** mentioned in each stanza does not refer to an earthly suitor but to Almighty God. The "me" to whom the gifts are presented refers to any baptized Catholic. The purpose of the repetition is not only for the sake of pedagogy but also emphasizes God's continual renewal of his gifts to mankind.

The **partridge** in a pear tree is Christ. In nature, a mother partridge will feign injury to lure predators away from her defenseless nestlings. In the same way, our Lord protects us, vulnerable human beings, from Satan. The pear tree symbolizes the cross, the instrument of salvation, just as the apple tree symbolizes Adam and Eve's Fall from Grace.

Two turtledoves represent the Old and New Testaments. The life of our Lord in its beginning is lived in the context of the covenant of the Old Testament. When St. Joseph and Mary presented baby Jesus in the Temple forty days after his birth, they offered two turtledoves as a sacrifice to God, the sacrifice of families of modest income instead of the customary lamb (see Lk 2:22–24). However, when Jesus begins his public ministry at his baptism in the River Jordan, we have the public revelation of the Trinity and the declaration that he is the Messiah and Son of God, thereby setting the context of the new covenant of the New Testament.

Known for their beauty and rarity, the **three French hens** signify both the gifts of the magi (gold, frankincense, and myrrh), and the three theological virtues of faith, hope, and charity.

The **four calling birds** are associated with both the four major prophets—Isaiah, Jeremiah, Ezekiel, and Daniel—and the four evangelists and their Gospels—Saints Matthew, Mark, Luke, and John. Here we have the prophets that prepared the way for the coming Messiah and the evangelists who proclaimed his Gospel. One could also include the four cardinal virtues—prudence, justice, fortitude, and temperance—and the four sets of Mysteries of the Rosary—Joyful, Luminous, Sorrowful, and Glorious.

The **five golden rings** have a two-fold significance. A ring, or a circle, has no beginning or end but is continuous. Thereby, the ring reminds us of both God's eternity, his permanent, faithful, and continuous love for us, and the circle of faith: God's love for us, our love for him, and our love for our neighbors. Moreover, gold is a pure element, and God's love is a pure, unconditional love.

The number five also signifies the first five books of the Old Testament—the Pentateuch, or Torah (the books of law for the Jewish people). The Torah taught the Jews how to live the covenant. Christ, who came to fulfill the Law and the prophets, established the new, perfect covenant. There are also five precepts of the Catholic Church.

The **six geese a-laying** represent the six days of creative work recounted in Genesis. God created everything "out of nothing," *ex nihilo*, with design, purpose, and order. Moreover, on the sixth day, God created man and woman in his divine image, instituted marriage, and blessed the procreation of children: "God created man in his image; in the divine image he created him; male and female he created them. God blessed them, saying: 'Be fertile and multiply; fill the earth and subdue it'" (Gn 1:27–8).

The **seven swans a-swimming** continues the Genesis theme. In Judaism, seven was a number of perfection. God's plan included not just the six days of creating but also the seventh day of rest; we, in turn, must not forget to make Sunday a holy day by worshiping God at Mass, spending time with our loved ones, and relaxing. Moreover, the seven swans a-swimming refers to the seven sacraments, the seven gifts of the Holy Spirit, the seven corporal works of mercy, and the seven spiritual works of mercy—all gifts and means to help us strive for Christian perfection and fulfill the Lord's command to "be perfect just as your heavenly Father is perfect" (Mt 5:48).

The **eight maids a-milking** signifies the eight beatitudes of the Sermon on the Mount (see Mt 5:1–12.)

The **nine ladies dancing** are the nine choirs of angels. The first three choirs see and adore God directly. The *seraphim*, whose name means "the burning ones," have the most intense "flaming" love for God and comprehend him with the greatest clarity. The *cherubim*, whose name means "fullness of wisdom," contemplate God's divine providence and plan for his creatures. And the *thrones*, symbolizing divine justice and judicial power, contemplate God's power and justice.

The next three choirs fulfill God's providential plan for the universe: The *dominations* or *dominions*, whose name evokes authority, govern the lesser choirs of angels. The *virtues*, whose name originally suggested power or strength, implement the orders from the dominations and govern the heavenly bodies. Lastly, the *powers* confront and fight against any evil forces opposed to God's providential plan.

The last three choirs are directly involved in human affairs: The *principalities* care for earthly principalities, such as nations or cities. The *archangels* deliver God's most important messages to mankind, while each *angel* serves as a guardian for each of us.

Although not official dogma, this schema of the nine choirs of angels became popular in the Middle Ages in the writings of St. Thomas Aquinas, Dante, Hildegard of Bingen, and John Scotus Erigina.

The Ten Commandments are represented by the **ten lords a-leaping**.

Eleven pipers piping are the eleven faithful apostles at the time of the Resurrection and Ascension. (Remember that Judas, one of the Twelve, betrayed our Lord and committed suicide.)

Finally, the number twelve for the Jewish people represented completion and fullness. Therefore, the **twelve drummers drumming** are the twelve minor prophets, the twelve precepts of the Apostles Creed (still the structure of the first part of the *Catechism*), the twelve apostles (the original eleven plus St. Matthias who replaced Judas), and the twelve tribes of Israel. Also, there are twelve Gifts of the Holy Spirit: charity, joy, peace, patience, kindness, goodness, generosity, gentleness, faithfulness, modesty, self-control, and chastity.

As we enjoy our Christmas celebration, we should keep in mind the significance of this carol. Actually, I used to find the repetition and lengthiness somewhat irritating until I learned of its historical and religious significance. A good practice would be for parents to teach the carol in light of the history of persecution and the catechesis presented. One could even have a family game night, for instance, where one thinks of the number, like seven, and then explains the significance of the number, like listing the seven sacraments. The winners, of course, could enjoy special treats.

The Christmas Tree

Each year, I look forward to decorating the Christmas tree in the rectory. Most of my ornaments are religious ones or have a special significance in my life. For example, I have an ornament that belonged to my maternal grandparents; on it, my grandmother taped a little note: "My Paul's and my first Christmas together, 1924." Only as a priest, though, did I come to know the significance of the Christmas tree.

The story of the Christmas tree is part of the story of the life of St. Boniface. St. Boniface was born about the year 680 in Devonshire, England. At the age of five, he wanted to become a monk and entered the monastery school near Exeter two years later. When he was fourteen, he entered the abbey of Nursling, in the Diocese of Winchester. Very studious himself, St. Boniface was the pupil of the learned abbot Winbert. Later, Boniface became the director of the school.

At this time, much of northern and central Europe still had not been evangelized. St. Boniface decided he wanted to be a missionary to these people. After one brief attempt, he sought the official approval of Pope St. Gregory II. The pope charged him with preaching the Gospel to the German people. St. Boniface traveled to Germany through the Alps into Bavaria.

In 722, the pope consecrated St. Boniface as a bishop with jurisdiction over all of Germany. Boniface knew that his greatest challenge was to eradicate pagan superstitions which hindered the acceptance of the Gospel and the conversion of the people. Known as "the Apostle to Germany," he would continue to preach the Gospel until he was martyred in 754. At this point, we can begin our story about the Christmas tree.

One Christmas Eve, St. Boniface was traveling with a band of his faithful monks through the woods along an old Roman road. The moon was full, and moonlight reflected brilliantly off the snow. They could see their breath in the crisp air. St. Boniface remembered his many happy days at his Benedictine abbey, especially during Christmas.

Although several monks suggested that they camp for the night, St. Boniface encouraged them to push forward, saying, "Courage, brothers. Just a short way to go. God's moon will light our way, and the path is plain. I know that you are weary. My own heart wearies also for the home in England, where those I love so dearly are making merry this Christmas Eve. But we have work to do before we feast tonight. For this is the Yule-tide, and the heathen people of the forest have gathered at the Thunder Oak of Geismar to worship Thor, the god of thunder and war. Strange things will be seen there, deeds which darken the soul. We are sent to bring light and shatter their darkness. We will teach our kinsmen about the truth of Christmas and the love of God. Forward, then, in the name of our Lord, Jesus Christ!"

St. Boniface's plea reinvigorated them, and they pushed ahead. After a while, the road opened to a clearing. They arrived at the village of Geismar. The homes were dark. Only the sounds of a few horses in the stable and the barking of dogs broke the quiet. In the distance, they heard voices.

As they followed a path through the woods, they came to a glade and there appeared the sacred Thunder Oak of Geismar. St. Boniface told his companions as he held his bishop's crozier high, "Here is the Thunder Oak, and here the cross of Christ shall break the hammer of the false god Thor."

In front of the tree was a huge bonfire. Sparks danced in the air. The townspeople surrounded the fire facing the Thunder Oak, listening to Hunrad, the priest of Thor. The crowd became quiet. St. Boniface assured them they had come in peace, and the monks were welcomed.

Hunrad then continued his preaching, "Stand still, common man, and behold what the gods have called us here to do! This night is the death-night of the sun-god, Baldur the Beautiful, beloved of gods and men. This night is the hour of darkness and the power of winter, of sacrifice and mighty fear. This night the great Thor, the god of thunder and war, to whom this oak is sacred, is grieved for the death of Baldur, and angry with this people because they have forsaken his worship. Long is it since an offering has been laid upon his altar, and the roots of his holy tree have been fed with blood. Therefore its leaves have withered before the time, and its boughs are heavy with death. And so, the Slavs and the Saxons have beaten us in battle. The harvests have failed. The cattle are infertile. Wolf-hordes and wild boars have attacked our hunters and killed our flocks. Sickness has fallen upon us, and many have died. Answer me, are not these things true?" The people sounded their approval and then began a chant of praise to Thor.

When the last sounds faded, Hunrad pronounced, "None of these chants will please the god. Only blood, the most costly of offerings, shall appease Thor, cleanse our sins, and send new life into this holy tree. Thor claims our dearest, most innocent, and our noblest gift."

With that, Hunrad approached the children grouped together around the fire. He selected the fairest boy, Asulf, the son of Duke Alvold and his wife, Thekla, and declared that he would be sacrificed to travel to Valhalla and bear the people's message to Thor. Asulf's parents were deeply shaken. Yet no one spoke.

Hunrad led the boy to a large stone altar between the oak and the fire. He blindfolded the child and had him kneel down, placing his head on the stone altar. The people moved closer, and St. Boniface positioned himself near the priest. Hunrad then lifted his sacred black-stone hammer of the god Thor high into the air, ready to have it crush little Asulf's skull. As Hunrad invoked Thor and was ready to bring down the hammer, St. Boniface thrust his crozier against the arm of Hunrad, and the hammer fell from his hand, splitting in two against the stone altar. Sounds of awe filled the air. St. Boniface said, "Untie the boy." Thekla ran to Asulf and embraced him tightly.

St. Boniface, his face radiant, then spoke to the people, "Tonight there will be no blood sacrifice. Tonight is the birth night of Jesus Christ, the son of the Almighty Father, the Savior of all mankind, who was born of the Virgin Mary, who had conceived by the Holy Spirit. He is the true God who became true man. He is life who conquers death. He is hope who conquers darkness and despair. He is truth who dispels error. He is love." Then holding high a crucifix, he said, "Here on this tree, this cross, Jesus poured forth the love of God—he offered his own life and shed his blood to the Father to forgive our sins, and he rose from the dead to open the gates of heaven and give us the hope of everlasting life. Jesus lives; Thor is dead." St. Boniface then took a broad ax and struck the

tree. Miraculously, a mighty wind suddenly arose and the tree fell, wrenching its roots from the earth, and split into four pieces.

Behind the mighty oak stood a young fir tree, pointing like a cathedral spire toward heaven. St. Boniface again spoke to the people. "This tree shall be your holy tree this night and every Christmas. It is the wood of peace, for your houses are built of the fir. It is the sign of everlasting life, for its leaves are evergreen. See how it points upward to heaven. Let this be called the tree of the Christchild, the true Savior and Lord of life. Gather about it, not in the wild wood, but in your own homes. There it will shelter gifts and acts of kindness."

So they cut down the fir tree and carried it to the village. Duke Alvold set the tree in the middle of his great hall. They placed candles on its branches, and it seemed filled with stars. Then St. Boniface, with Hunrad sitting at his feet, told the story of Christmas. All listened intently. Little Asulf, sitting on his mother's lap, said,

"Mother, listen now, for I hear those angels singing again behind the tree." Some say it was so, while some say it was St. Boniface's companions singing. Nevertheless, the words were taken to heart: "Glory to God in the highest, and on earth, peace to men of good will."

A Spiritual Opportunity

As we gather around our Christmas trees this year, may we give thanks for the gift of our Faith, hold the story of our Savior's birth in our hearts, and listen for the song of the angels. Remembering St. Boniface, take time to read the story of Christmas and sing joyful carols around the tree at home.

As we gaze at the Christmas tree, let us consider our own lives and the gifts we offer Jesus. We too live in a secular, pagan world that can seem so dark at times. Nevertheless, we are called to be like the Christmas tree.

First, the fir tree has deep roots and a strong trunk and it reaches to heaven. St. Paul exhorted, "Be rooted in him and built upon him, and established in the faith as you were taught" (Col 2:7). We must be rooted in the truth—the truth we find the Bible, Sacred Scripture; in the teachings of the Church, our *Catechism*; and in the lives of the saints, for they were and are lights shining in the darkness.

We need to have a strong trunk. Let us not bend to the winds of popular opinion but remain strong. St. Paul taught, "Do not conform yourselves to this age, but be transformed by the renewal of your mind, that you may discern what is the will of God, what is good and pleasing and perfect" (Rom 12:2).

We need to reach to the heavens, remembering that is our eternal home. St. Paul said, "Seek what is above, where Christ is seated

at the right hand of God" (Col 3:1). We must not become distracted by the things of this world and the pursuit of some worldly kingdom, for all those things pass away and are left behind in a grave. Therefore, notice how the fir tree is triangular. It shows our priorities—God comes first, then marriage, then family, and then everything else. Just as a fir tree cannot grow and live upside down, neither can we. If we keep the priorities straight in this life, we will enjoy everlasting life.

Second, the fir tree has branches which reach out and upwards and are very supple. Our arms need to reach upwards through daily prayer and worship at Holy Mass. Christ came into this world to share his life with us, but we have to open our hearts to share our lives with him. He does not force himself upon us. Take time for daily prayer and Holy Mass—how else can we have a friendship with the Lord and know his love?

Just as the arms of Mary presented the infant Jesus to the shepherds and the magi, we need to present Jesus to others and lead others to Jesus. Just as the strong arms of St. Joseph provided for his family and others, our arms must care for those entrusted to us, and reach out to those who are the poor, the needy, the suffering, the forgotten, the elderly.

Just as the fir tree's branches are supple, bending when weighed down with snow but bouncing back, we must be supple. We at times may carry great burdens that weigh us down. If we share those burdens with the Lord and keep our eyes fixed on him, we will bounce back, we will not break. Jesus said, "Come to me all you who labor and are burdened, and I will give you rest. Take my yoke upon you and learn from me, for I am meek and humble of heart; and you will find rest for your selves. For my yoke is easy, and my burden light" (Mt 11:29–30).

Third, just as the fir tree is evergreen, we must remember the everlasting life that the Lord offers. That life, however, begins now, especially through the Holy Eucharist. Jesus said, "I am the living bread that came down from heaven; whoever eats this bread, will live forever; and the bread I will give is my flesh for the life of the world. . . . Whoever eats my flesh and drinks my blood has eternal life, and I will raise him on the last day" (Jn 6:51, 54). At every Mass, Christ does come to us. We offer the sacrifice that participates in the everlasting sacrifice of our Lord. Bread and wine are transubstantiated into the Body, Blood, Soul, and Divinity of our Lord. He comes to give us the promise and foretaste of everlasting life. Always remember Christmas means "Christ's Mass" and that is really every Mass. Every Mass is Christmas, and we receive the greatest gift of all, Jesus himself.

We learn much from our Christmas tree. Take its meaning to heart. St. Boniface gave us a great gift and instituted a wonderful tradition. His name in Latin comes from *Bonus Fatum*, meaning "good fate." Let us lift up grateful hearts to the Lord this Christmas for the gift of our Savior and look forward to our everlasting life in heaven.

Christmas Greenery and Plants

Some of our Christian Christmas decorations of greenery and plants originated from pagan customs. Nevertheless, with the evangelization of the pagan peoples by the missionaries, these decorations were "baptized," giving them a new Christian meaning. Let us consider the five common Christmas decorations: mistletoe, holly, ivy, laurel, and poinsettias.

Mistletoe, holly, ivy, and laurel are evergreens. Whether in a pagan or Christian culture, evergreens have symbolized eternity and everlasting life. For Christians in particular, the evergreens have the symbolism that our Lord is eternal and divine, and that he wants us to share his everlasting life in the kingdom of heaven.

The **mistletoe** was regarded as a magical healing plant by the pagan Druids. It was even called "All heal." The Christians adopted this plant and now it is a symbol of Christ, the Divine Healer of all nations. In the Gospels, we find many healing stories of our Lord, but most importantly, he came to heal the wound of our sin.

As far as the "kissing" associated with mistletoe, an ancient Norse legend relates that Freya, the goddess of love, placed mistletoe in a tree between heaven and earth, and decided that people who pass underneath it should kiss. The plant then became a sign of love and friendship. While love and friendship are definitely Christian virtues to be practiced, I don't think that random kissing is the intent of the Christmas decoration. Nevertheless, God is love, and Jesus fully revealed that love to us; any kissing underneath the mistletoe, therefore, ought to reflect true Christian love.

The Roman god Bacchus, the god of wine, wore **ivy** in his crown. (Also, his cult was associated with debauchery, a word derived from his name.) For this reason, the early Christians did not use ivy inside the church to decorate, but it was used outside as a Christmas decoration. Ivy grows upward, clinging to something, like a wall or a trellis. The vines are rather fragile and can break easily. For Christians, the ivy reminds us that we were weakened due to Original Sin and could not save ourselves. Christ came to save us. We must faithfully cling to our Lord, relying on his strength to be holy and to climb upward to heaven to attain salvation.

While not known for sure, some sources hold that the pagan Romans sent **holly** branches as a sign of good wishes at the time of the new year's festivals. The early Christians easily saw a more profound symbolism: the prickly, sharp points of the leaves symbolize the crown of thorns and even the nails of the Crucifixion, and the red berries symbolize the blood that flowed from our Lord's wounds. The holly decoration at Christmas thereby reminds us that Christ was born to suffer and die for our sins, which would be washed away with his precious blood. For this reason, in Norway and Sweden, the holly is called "Christ-thorn."

Some traditional stories surround the holly tree. One is told that when the Holy Family was fleeing King Herod's soldiers, they took refuge under a holly tree which spread its branches, thick with leaves, to protect them. The sharp, pointed leaves would have driven away any sensible person from searching, thereby safely concealing the Holy Family. For this action, our Blessed Mother blessed the tree and said it would be perpetually green.

Another legend is that the cross was made from holly wood. Because of this connection with our Lord's passion and death—his crown of thorns and shedding of blood—the tree was marked thereafter with sharp, pointed leaves and blood-red berries.

In the carol *The Holly and the Ivy*, two other symbols of holly are noted: First, the holly blossom is white "as the lily flower," reminding us of the purity of Jesus born of his mother, Mary; and second, the holly bark, "as bitter as any gall," reminds us of the drink offered our Lord as he hung upon the cross. The traditional lyrics are as follows:

> The holly and the ivy,
> When they are both full grown,
> Of all the trees that are in the wood,
> The holly bears the crown.

> *Chorus*
> The rising of the sun
> And the running of the deer,
> The playing of the merry organ,
> Sweet singing in the choir.

> The holly bears a blossom,
> As white as the lily flower,
> And Mary bore sweet Jesus Christ,
> To be our sweet Savior.

Chorus

The holly bears a berry,
As red as any blood,
And Mary bore sweet Jesus Christ
For to do us sinners good.

Chorus

The holly bears a prickle,
As sharp as any thorn,
And Mary bore sweet Jesus Christ
On Christmas Day in the morn.

Chorus

The holly bears a bark,
As bitter as any gall,
And Mary bore sweet Jesus Christ
For to redeem us all.

Chorus

The holly and the ivy,
When they are both full grown,
Of all the trees that are in the wood,
The holly bears the crown.

Chorus

The last evergreen is laurel. Roman emperors used **laurel** leaves to form a wreath to be worn on the head as a sign of victory. Such laurel crowns were also awarded to military leaders who were victorious in battle and to athletes who had won contests. The virgins of the goddess Vesta also considered laurel sacred and a sign of virtue.

At Christmastime, laurel reminds us of Christ's victory over sin and death, and our call to holiness. We hope to attain the crown of victory over sin and reign with our Lord in heaven. St. Paul taught, "The runners in the stadium all run in the race, but only one wins the prize. Run so as to win! Every athlete exercises discipline in every way. They do it to win an imperishable crown, but we an imperishable one" (1 Cor 9:24–25). In writing to St. Timothy before the end of his life, St. Paul again used the same imagery: "The time of my departure is at hand. I have competed well; I have finished the race; I have kept the faith. From now on the crown of righteousness awaits me, which the Lord, the just judge, will award to me on that day, and not only to me, but to all who have longed for his appearance" (2 Tm 4:7–8).

The **poinsettia**, a native plant of Central America, is also very popular. The bright red leaves symbolize the burning, divine love of our Redeemer. The shape of the cluster of leaves and the contrast of the red with the green also remind one of the star of Bethlehem that shone so brightly the night our Savior was born and then guided the magi to visit him.

A popular legend surrounds the poinsettia. Long ago, on Christmas Eve, Maria, a little girl in Mexico, wanted to bring a gift to Baby Jesus, lying in the crèche at her church. Maria's family was very poor. She could not buy a gift, as the other children of the town did. She did not even expect a gift herself for Christmas.

On the way to church for Christmas Mass, she was feeling very sad. As she walked along the road, she saw a very green bushy plant. She thought, "I will give this to Baby Jesus." She uprooted the plant, wrapped it in her scarf, and carried it to church.

When she arrived at church, the whole congregation looked at her. Some people chuckled at this little girl with her plant as she walked up the aisle and approached the altar where the nativity scene was. Some scoffed and frowned. One said in an audible voice, "Look at the Indian who brought a weed for Jesus."

As she went up the aisle, she became more and more self-conscious and began to cry. At the altar rail, she tearfully handed the plant to Padre Joseph, a very kind priest who smiled at her because he knew this was the best she could give. He took the plant in one hand and, with the other, held Maria's hand. Together, they walked towards the manger scene.

When Padre Joseph placed the plant right next to Jesus in the crib, all were amazed: the green leaves had turned a beautiful red. Some people said with astonishment, "A miracle!" Maria's face lit up with great joy. Padre Joseph said, "Look. These bright red leaves against the green are like the star of Bethlehem that shone so brightly the night our Savior was born, guiding the Magi to visit him. They show the burning, divine love of our Redeemer and the blood he shed for us."

Little Maria had given the best gift of all, the gift of her innocent, genuine love. Since then, the poinsettia has been a traditional Christmas plant and is called in Mexico the "flower of the Good Night," *la flor de Nochebuena*. It reminds us of the most beautiful exchange of gifts: that between God and us.

Such greenery and plants have a beautiful meaning for Christians. As we decorate our homes this year, let us look upon them as reminders of the real meaning of Christmas.

The Christmas Crèche

The story of the origin of the Christmas crèche rests with the very holy man St. Francis of Assisi. In the year 1223, St. Francis, a deacon, was visiting the town of Greccio to celebrate Christmas. Greccio was a small town built on a mountainside overlooking a beautiful valley. The people had cultivated the fertile area with vineyards. St. Francis realized that the chapel of the Franciscan hermitage would be too small to hold the congregation for midnight Mass, so he set up the altar in the town square.

To make this Christmas celebration even more memorable, St. Francis wanted to depict the first Christmas scene. He borrowed an ox and an ass from a farmer and set up a manger. He also placed there the statues of St. Joseph and the Blessed Mother along with a little baby doll to serve as Jesus. Truly, he thought, this midnight Mass would be very special, unlike any other.

St. Bonaventure (d. 1274), in his *The Life of St. Francis of Assisi*, tells the story the best:

It happened in the third year before his death, that in order to excite the inhabitants of Greccio to commemorate the nativity of

the Infant Jesus with great devotion, [St. Francis] determined to keep it with all possible solemnity; and lest he should be accused of lightness or novelty, he asked and obtained the permission of the sovereign Pontiff. Then he prepared a manger, and brought hay, and an ox and an ass to the place appointed. The brethren were summoned, the people ran together, the forest resounded with their voices, and that venerable night was made glorious by many and brilliant lights and sonorous psalms of praise. The man of God [St. Francis] stood before the manger, full of devotion and piety, bathed in tears and radiant with joy; the Holy Gospel was chanted by Francis, the Levite of Christ. Then he preached to the people around the nativity of the poor King; and being unable to utter His Name for the tenderness of His love, he called Him the Babe of Bethlehem. A certain valiant and veracious soldier, Master John of Greccio, who, for the love of Christ, had left the warfare of this world, and became a dear friend of this holy man, affirmed that he beheld an Infant marvelously beautiful, sleeping in the manger, Whom the blessed Father Francis embraced with both his arms, as if he would awake Him from sleep. This vision of the devout soldier is credible, not only by reason of the sanctity of him that saw it, but by reason of the miracles which afterwards confirmed its truth. For the example of Francis, if it be considered by the world, is doubtless sufficient to excite all hearts which are negligent in the faith of Christ; and the hay of that manger, being preserved by the people, miraculously cured all diseases of cattle, and many other pestilences; God thus in all things glorifying his servant and witnessing to the great efficacy of his holy prayers by manifest prodigies and miracles.

Although the story is very old, the message is clear for us. The nativity scenes which rest under our own Christmas trees are a visible reminder of that night when our Savior was born. May we never forget to see in our hearts the little Babe of Bethlehem, who came to save us from sin. We must never forget that the wood of the manger that held him so securely would one day give way to the wood of the cross. Interestingly, almost one year later, on September 14, 1224, on the Feast of the Holy Cross, St. Francis received the stigmata, the first saint known to have this privilege; he who held the baby Jesus with such tender love also bore his wounds. This Christmas, may we too embrace our Lord with all our love and devotion as did St. Francis of Assisi.

A Meditation

While our own nativity scene may be more elaborate than that of St. Francis, we ought to meditate on the various figures and elements. Most importantly, we gaze upon the baby **Jesus**. In the fullness of time, God sent his Son not to condemn the world, but to give everlasting life to those who believe (see Jn 3:16). Yes, Jesus, second person of the Holy Trinity, consubstantial with the Father, entered this world through Mary, a Virgin, full of grace, who had conceived by the Holy Spirit. True God became also true man. As St. John wrote, "The Word became flesh and made his dwelling among us, and we saw his glory, the glory as of the Father's only Son, full of grace and truth" (Jn 1:14). He came not as a powerful king with an army of angels to conquer and force us to believe; rather, he came as a baby to disarm us with love. For who does not love a baby? Who does not want to hold a baby? Who does not cast off adult pretenses when holding a baby?

While we gaze at baby Jesus, we must always look up—for there we see Jesus the man, with arms outstretched, who perfectly revealed God's truth and love, who took the burden of all sin unto himself and offered the perfect sacrifice that transcends time, so that each person can say, "Jesus died for my sins and rose to give me the hope of everlasting life."

Jesus also entered our circumstances—marriage, family, and home. He was born of **Mary** and entrusted to **St. Joseph**, his foster father, who was a righteous man. They loved God most of all and did his will. They loved each other as husband and wife and were devoted parents. As a Jewish father and husband, St. Joseph was the good masculine example for Jesus. He provided for his family, even if this time the best he could find was the shelter of a stable. He guarded them from the wrath of King Herod. He was the spiritual leader who led the family in prayer each morning and evening, before meals, who took them to the synagogue for the Sabbath or Jerusalem for special feast days. He taught Jesus to read, especially to read the Torah. What a great gift St. Joseph was to Jesus! What a great gift any father like St. Joseph is to his wife and children!

Mary too was that special mother. Prepared from the first moment of her life (her Immaculate Conception), she was full of grace and free of all sin, even the stain of Original Sin. She freely said yes to God and conceived by the power of the Holy Spirit. Like any mother, Mary must have been the heart of the home. We can imagine all the good things Mary did, as any mom would. What a great gift Mary was to Jesus! What a great gift any mother like Mary is to her husband and children.

Husbands and wives, mothers and fathers, be such a gift to your children. Make Christ the Lord of your lives and your home. Nurture in them a Catholic Christian identity and teach them how to live as Catholic Christians. Make your home an extension of the Church.

Children, cherish the gift of your family and your home.

Others were present as well. Simple **shepherds**, living off the land, sought the child. They had a child-like quality—trust, innocence, and dependence. Remember what Jesus said to the apostles who asked, "Who is the greatest in the kingdom of heaven?" He answered that "unless you . . . become like children, you will not enter the kingdom of heaven. Whoever humbles himself like this child is the greatest in the kingdom of heaven" (Mt 18:1–4).

How appropriate, too, that the Good Shepherd would first gather the shepherds as the first sheep of the flock, the first witnesses of the newborn Savior: "All who heard of [the birth of the Messiah] were astonished at the report given them by the shepherds" (see Lk 2:8–20).

Guided by a star, the **magi**—wise men—came from the East bearing gifts: gold for a king, frankincense for a priest, and myrrh, a burial ointment for one who would die. They were wise, but wise enough to know they did not know everything. They prostrated themselves and adored. Where the accumulation of money, power, material things, and social activities can make us anxious and consume our lives, a return to a simpler life would free us of such burdens. After they adored, they returned to their own country by another route (see Mt 2:12), avoiding wicked King Herod. We too are called to reorient our lives to Christ, follow his path, and avoid the near occasion of sin. Proverbs 3:5–6 captures the message well: "Trust in the Lord with all your heart, on your own intelligence rely not; in all your ways be mindful of him, and he will make straight your paths." Is Christ the "star" who guides us on our journey of life, and is our heart open to follow him? (More will be discussed on this topic when we meditate on the Epiphany.)

The shepherds and the magi prompt us to ask ourselves, "How much do we really need?" In a world of technology and science, when some think they are so enlightened they do not think of God and even the notion of God offends them, we need to humble ourselves. We have achieved power over life and death without conscience; we have become technological giants but ethical and moral infants. Now is the time to turn our hearts back to the wisdom of God and to cast aside the political ideology for Gospel truth.

The nativity reminds us that there were the **animals** too. They were part of God's creation. **Sheep** were raised for wool, so each was precious. They were also raised for the Temple sacrifices, like those at Passover. Sheep came to adore the Good Shepherd who himself came to gather us into the Church, his flock, and into God's love. We too must remember that each of us is precious in the eyes of the Lord, and we are a member of the flock, the Catholic Church that our Lord founded upon the apostles.

Sheep were raised for sacrifice, and St. John the Baptist identified Jesus as the Lamb of God. Jesus said, "I am sending you like sheep in the midst of wolves" (Mt 10:16). Yes, there are those who would like to devour us, as they did the martyrs; nevertheless, we are called to be martyrs, witnesses of the Faith for others. And like the martyrs, we must cast off fear, for Jesus promised to be with us "until the end of the world" (Mt 28:20). To be effective witnesses, we need to know and to cherish our Faith, for we cannot share what we do not have.

The little sheep remind us, too, that Jesus came to go after the lost sheep, for sheep easily become distracted and wander for what seems to be greener pastures. At Christmastime especially, we ought to pray for the lost sheep in our own families and look for the graced opportunities to encourage them to return to the flock.

Then there were the **ox** and the **ass**, two traditional parts of our nativity scene. We read in Isaiah that "the ox knows its owner, and the ass its master's crib" (1:3). This prophecy foretold the new people of God, the Church consisting of both Jews and Gentiles. Also, the ox reminds us of what Jesus said: that we must take his yoke upon your shoulders and learn from him, and that in doing so our souls will find rest, for his yoke is easy and his burden light (see Mt 11:29–30). The yoke was custom made to fit a particular ox, and a pair of oxen were harnessed together for plowing. The ox reminds us that we are called to do his work, but that he will help us along the way.

The donkey was the beast of burden that carried our blessed Mother to Bethlehem and carried Jesus into Jerusalem on Palm Sunday. A tradition is that the donkey of Palm Sunday followed Jesus to Calvary. As he hung upon the cross, the donkey bowed down. The shadow of the cross left a dark streak from ear to ear and down the back of the donkey, a reminder that Jesus said that we must, each of us, take up our cross and follow him (see Mt 16:24). The ox and the ass remind us that we are called to serve the Lord and to serve him in others, alleviating the burden of our fellow man, knowing that we are not alone but that he is always with us.

We also have an **angel**—and the Gospel says there was a multitude of angels. Remember, we have our guardian angel, whom we should rely on for help "to light, to guard, to rule, and to guide," as we pray in the "Guardian Angel prayer."

What about the straw, the **hay**? It provided warmth, food, and comfort. There is an Eastern European tradition that if a person carries a piece of straw in his wallet or her purse, there will always be enough warmth, food, and comfort to sustain him or her for the entire year.

Have we missed anything? What about the **manger** itself? The manger contained hay for the animals to eat. Jesus is the Bread of Life who came to feed us with his very life. Jesus said, "I am the living bread that came down from heaven; whoever eats this bread will live forever; and the bread that I will give is my flesh for the life of the world. . . . Whoever eats my flesh and drinks my blood has eternal life, and I will raise him up on the last day. For my flesh is true food, and my blood is true drink. Whoever eats my flesh and drinks my blood remains in me and I in him" (Jn 6:51, 54–56). Remember, too, that *Bethlehem,* where Jesus was born, means "House of Bread."

Yes, Jesus feeds us with his very life through the Holy Eucharist. In a way, the manger is like the altar on which our Lord in the Holy Eucharist rests. Like St. Francis, who held baby Jesus one Christmas Eve at Midnight Mass, we can hold him in our heart when we receive the Holy Eucharist.

As you can see, it is well worthwhile to reflect upon and teach the children the significance of the different parts of the crèche.

Christmas Candles

The tradition of placing lit candles in the windows arises from the British persecution against the Catholic Church in Ireland. Since the time King Henry II invaded Ireland in 1171, the Irish have been persecuted. This persecution increased tremendously in the wake of the Protestant movement, especially under Elizabeth I and then Oliver Cromwell. They believed that they must control the religion of the people in order to rule. The British conquerors were Protestant and the Irish people were Catholic; therefore, to totally subjugate the Irish people, the British decided they had to crush their religion, and that meant crushing the Catholic Church.

This persecution was formalized and promulgated in what were known as the Penal Laws. The statesman Edmund Burke wrote,

> All the penal laws of that unparalleled code of oppression were manifestly the effects of national hatred and scorn toward a conquered people whom the victors delighted to trample upon and were not at all afraid to provoke. They were not the effect of their fears, but of their security . . . whilst that temper prevailed, and

it prevailed in all its force to a time within our memory, every measure was pleasing and popular just in proportion as it tended to harass and ruin a set of people who were looked upon as enemies of God and man; indeed, as a race of savages, who were a disgrace to human nature itself.

With the rise of King William III and Queen Mary II, the penal laws were perfected. They were designed to eradicate Catholicism by making the practice of the Faith too burdensome. As I observed earlier, Catholic clergy were ordered to leave the country by May 1, 1698; if after that date they were found remaining, they would be imprisoned and then exiled; and if they returned, they would be liable to being hanged unconscious, drawn (disemboweled while alive), and quartered (beheaded and cut into four pieces). Catholics were forbidden to practice the Faith, attend Mass, send a child to a Catholic teacher, send a child to a Catholic school abroad, hold public office, engage in commerce, live in a corporate town, purchase or lease land, vote, or hold arms for protection. Punishments for violations included confiscation of goods, fines, imprisonment, exile, and even death. Burke commented in his *Tract on the Popery Code*: "There was not a single right of nature or benefit of society which had not been either totally taken away or considerably impaired." Even Chief Justice Robinson, during the reign of George I, stated, "The law does not suppose any such person to exist as an Irish Roman Catholic."

Despite this persecution, the Catholic Faith kept the Irish strong. Bishops and priests continued to minister to the people, traveling circuits and offering Mass on "Mass rocks" in open fields. Hiding behind hedges, which provided easy lookout and escape, schoolmasters continued to teach the children, not just regular studies, but also the Faith and their Irish heritage; they were thereby called "hedge schoolmasters." With great fortitude, the Irish people held true to their Faith and culture.

Here we come to the use of candles in the windows. During Christmas, every faithful Irish Catholic family hoped to have a priest visit their home so that they could receive the sacraments and offer him hospitality in return. They would leave their doors unlocked and place candles in the windows to signal a priest that he was welcome and would be safe. Sometimes, a single candle would appear in windows, others three candles in one window, to represent Jesus, Mary, and Joseph.

Of course, the British persecutors became suspicious and asked the purpose of this action. The faithful Irish Catholics simply responded, "Our doors are unlocked and candles burn in our windows at Christmas, so that our Blessed Mother Mary, St. Joseph, and baby Jesus, looking for a place to lodge, will find their way to our homes and be welcomed with open hearts." The British naturally considered such a display another sign of superstition and "silly popery."

Here, then, is the origin of this custom, which is still cherished by the Irish. The custom of placing candles in the windows was brought to America by Irish immigrants and has since become very popular. Nevertheless, we must never lose sight of its meaning and historical background.

A Meditation

Christ is our light who entered this world to scatter sin and darkness. Jesus said, "I am the light of the world" (Jn 9:5). Having been enlightened by Christ through Holy Baptism, we must have a strong loyalty to our Church. Remember that the priest, shortly after the baptism of pouring of water and invoking the Holy

Trinity, presented to us or our godparent a candle lit from the Pascal Candle, saying, "Receive the light of Christ. You have been enlightened by Christ. Walk always as a child of that light. May you always keep the flame of faith alive in your heart. When the Lord comes, may you go out to meet him with all the saints in the heavenly kingdom."

At Christmas, we too must realize that the greatest gift of all is our Faith, a faith which enabled the Irish to triumph over the most heinous persecutions. We too must always remember to be the light of the world. Recalling the instruction at our baptism, we must keep the flame of faith alive in our hearts until the Day of the Lord. Through our lives, we must be the light that penetrates and dispels the darkness of evil. Consider that if a room were totally dark, one single candle would break the darkness and provide direction. Consider also that from one lit candle, a multitude of candles could be lit. We must be the light that conquers darkness and direct others to Christ. We must hand on the flame of faith to others.

Silent Night, Holy Night

My favorite Christmas carol is *Silent Night*, and I came to appreciate it more when I knew the story of its origin.

The story of *Silent Night* begins in the beautiful city of Salzburg, Austria. In the splendor of that baroque city ruled by the prince archbishop, lived a simple weaver named Anna. Anna, alone in this world, was of very modest means with little hope of raising her lifestyle or even marrying. One day she fell in love with a soldier stationed in Salzburg. In a fling of passion, she and the soldier conceived a child, who was born on December 11, 1792. However, he took no responsibility for his child and left Anna and the baby to fend for themselves. Nevertheless, Anna gave the soldier's surname, Mohr, to her baby, whom she named "Joseph," trusting that the foster father of our Lord, St. Joseph, would look after and guard him. Being an unwed mother with a child born out of wedlock, Anna knew the scorn and rejection of society. As a last resort, she asked the city hangman to be the godparent to her baby Joseph.

Anna provided as best she could for Joseph. She realized that a good education would give him the hope of a good future. The local

Mohr. Gruber.

tille Nacht, heilige Nacht! Wer hat Dich, o Lied, gemacht
Mohr hat mich so schön erdacht, Gruber zu G...

parish priest recognized young Joseph's brightness and his singing ability. He arranged for him to attend the famous abbey school of Kremsmunster. There, young Joseph excelled in his studies. He later realized he had a vocation to the priesthood and entered the seminary at the age of sixteen. When he was ready for ordination at the age of twenty-two, Joseph needed a special dispensation, since he had no father.

Joseph Mohr was assigned as the assistant pastor at St. Nicholas Church in Oberndorf, about ten miles northwest of Salzburg on the River Salzach. (The church of St. Nicholas was destroyed by flooding in 1899, but a memorial chapel stands there today.) The parish was of very modest means, and the pastor was strict and frugal to say the least.

Here, Father Mohr became friends with Franz Gruber. Gruber was the son of a weaver, who had little appreciation for music. Franz was expected to follow in the trade of his father. Despite his father's disapproval, Franz began playing the guitar and the organ. The parish priest allowed Franz even to practice his music in church. His talents eventually were recognized, and he was sent to school for formal musical training. He eventually settled in the town of Oberndorf, working as a music teacher and raising his family of twelve children. Mohr and Gruber shared their love of music, and both played the guitar.

On December 23, 1818, with Christmas fast approaching, Father Mohr went to visit a mother and her newborn child. On the way back to the rectory, he paused by the river and meditated on the first Christmas. The sky was filled with stars and the light of the moon made the river twinkle with light. He pondered the Gospel Christmas story, on which he would preach at midnight Mass. He thought of how his own life fit into the Christmas story. Like Jesus, he was blessed with a loving mother like Mary and good spiritual fathers like St. Joseph, after whom he was named. Like Jesus who was born in a stable, he was born into poverty; but just as that stable was filled with love, so was his home, and that is all that mattered.

He was surrounded by insignificant members of society, just as Jesus was surrounded by shepherds. But as a priest, he learned those considered "insignificant" often have the greatest faith because they need God more. In the eyes of God, everyone is significant and precious, for God has given the gift of life to each.

Times were tough, just as they were at the time of Jesus. Many were unemployed; many had lost their lives in the Napoleonic wars; there was political unrest; and, sadly, many had stopped practicing the Faith. He realized, though, and believed that on the first Christmas a beautiful light had come into this world that no darkness could ever extinguish. This was the light that enlightened his own life. This light was Jesus.

With that meditation, he penned the words to a poem he called *Silent Night, Holy Night*. He captured in his composition the ineffable mystery of the incarnation and birth of our Lord, the holy infant Jesus, who is Christ the Son of God, Love's Pure Light, Lord, and Savior.

Jesus is the **Son of God** and **Love's Pure Light**. He is the second person of the Holy Trinity, the Word of God, and the Wisdom of God. As we profess in the Nicene Creed, he is "the Only Begotten Son of God, born of the Father before all ages. God from God, Light from Light, true God from true God, begotten not made, consubstantial with the Father; through him all things were made." By the will of the Father, Jesus entered this world, becoming also true man through Mary, who conceived by the power of the Holy Spirit.

Jesus is the **Lord.** Through him, all things were created. He is Lord over physical creation, who changed water into wine, raised the dead, calmed the storm, and cured the sick, the blind, and the lame. He is also the Lord over spiritual creation, who forgave sins, exorcized demons, and healed the brokenhearted.

Jesus is the **Savior.** Only he, true God who became also true man, could offer the perfect sacrifice to forgive ours sins that transcends time—for sins of the past, his time, our time. And he rose, offering redeeming grace and everlasting life.

Yes, the verses of a simple poem captured an ineffable mystery!

Returning to the parish, he was confronted with the news that the organ was broken. Voracious mice had eaten through the bellows needed to produce music. Being so close to Christmas and without sufficient funds to consider repairing the organ, the people feared that midnight Mass would be silent. Father Mohr rushed to the home of his friend Franz Gruber and shared his plight. He handed Gruber the poem and asked him to write a melody for it to be played on the guitar. Franz Gruber completed the task in time. At midnight Mass, 1818, the world heard for the first time the simple yet profound song we know as *Silent Night*.

The song was well received and quickly spread throughout Austria, oftentimes being called simply *A Tyrolean Carol*. Frederick Wilhelm IV, King of Prussia, heard *Silent Night* at the Berlin Imperial Church and ordered it to be sung throughout the kingdom at Christmas pageants and services. Ironically, the music gained fame without any attribution to its composers. Some thought Michael Haydn, the brother of the famous composer Franz Joseph Haydn, wrote the piece. Frederick Wilhelm, thereby, ordered a search.

One day, the king's agents arrived at St. Peter's monastery in Salzburg inquiring about the composers of *Silent Night*. Felix, the son of Franz Gruber, who was a student there, approached them and told them the story behind *Silent Night*. He directed them to his father, who was now the choirmaster of another parish. From that time on, both Mohr and Gruber were credited with *Silent Night*.

Since then, the simple carol *Silent Night* has been translated into countless languages and sung around the world by the faithful.

Our English translation is attributed to John Freeman Young and Jane Montgomery Campbell. Take to heart the words of *Silent Night* and proclaim its message in thought, word, and deed.

Silent Night

Silent night! Holy night!
All is calm, all is bright
'Round yon virgin mother and child!
Holy infant, so tender and mild,
Sleep in heavenly peace,
Sleep in heavenly peace.

Silent night! Holy night!
Shepherds quake at the sight.
Glories stream from heaven afar,
Heav'nly hosts sing: "Alleluia!
Christ the Savior is born!
Christ the Savior is born!"

Silent night! Holy night!
Son of God, love's pure light
Radiant beams from Thy holy face
With the dawn of redeeming grace,
Jesus, Lord, at Thy birth!
Jesus, Lord, at Thy birth!

Silent night! Holy night!
Wondrous star, lend thy light;
With the angels let us sing
"Alleluia" to our King:
"Christ the Savior is born!
Christ the Savior is born."

December 25,
The Birthdate of Jesus

All people remember and celebrate their birthdays. Yet some ask, "How do we know that Jesus was born on December 25? How wonderful it would be if our Lord had been born in the age of information technology or even when the public records office issued birth certificates! Alas, the Gospels do not provide such information. Nevertheless, some scriptural detective work can help determine the date of Christ's birth.

St. Luke related the announcement of the birth of St. John the Baptist to his elderly parents, St. Zechariah and St. Elizabeth. St. Zechariah was a priest of the class of Abijah (see Lk 1:5), the eighth class of twenty-four priestly classes (see Neh 12:17). Each class served one week in the Temple, twice a year.

Josef Heinrich Friedlieb has established that the priestly class of Abijah would have been on duty during the second week of the Jewish month Tishri, the week of the Day of Atonement or, in our calendar, between September 22 and 30. While on duty, the archangel Gabriel informed St. Zechariah that he and his wife would have a son. Thereupon, they conceived John, who after presumably forty weeks in the womb would have been born at the end of June. For this reason, we celebrate the Nativity of St. John the Baptist on June 24.

St. Luke also recorded how the archangel Gabriel told Mary that her cousin, St. Elizabeth, was six months pregnant with St. John (see Lk 1:36), which means the Annunciation occurred on March 25, as we celebrate. Nine months from March 25, or six months from June 24· renders the birth of Christ at December 25, our date for Christmas.

On a pious note, would not our Blessed Mother herself have remembered these details, especially how she conceived by the Holy Spirit and bore the Savior? Surely. All mothers—including my own—remember these details. Would not the apostles have asked her these questions, at least after the Ascension? Would not St. Luke, who included the details of the Annunciation and Visitation, have learned them from our Blessed Mother? Pope Benedict, in his book *Jesus of Nazareth: The Infancy Narratives*, noted this very point:

> Luke indicates from time to time that Mary, the Mother of Jesus, is herself one of his sources, especially when he says in 2:51 that "His mother kept all these things in her heart." Only she could report the event of the Annunciation, for which there were no human witnesses. . . . To sum up: what Matthew and Luke set out to do, each in his own way, was not to tell 'stories' but to write history, real history that had actually happened, admittedly interpreted and understood in the context of the word of God." (pp. 16–17)

Given the facts of the Gospel, then, we can discover the date of Christmas.

Now if this dating is true, then the early Church must have celebrated Christmas on December 25. Is there evidence? Admittedly, evidence is sparse because Christianity and the Church were persecuted by the Roman Empire until the year 313, and no one knows how much evidence has been lost. Nevertheless, according to the *Liber pontificalis*, Pope St. Telesphorus (125–136) instituted the tradition of celebrating midnight Mass, which means Christmas was already being celebrated. St. Theophilus (115–181), Bishop of Caesarea, stated, "We ought to celebrate the birthday of Our Lord on what day so ever the 25th of December shall happen." St. Hippolytus (170–240) mentioned in his *Commentary on Daniel* that the birth of Christ occurred on December 25.

After Constantine legalized Christianity in the year 313, the Church was able to establish universal dates for the celebration of feast days, including Christmas and the Annunciation. As such, evidence shows the celebration of Christmas on December 25: Pope Liberius (352–366) celebrated Christmas Mass in Rome; St. Gregory Nazianzus (d. 389) in Constantinople, and St. Ambrose (d. 397) in Milan. Keep in mind that they would not have just "picked a date" but used the date already accepted by the Church.

So what about Christmas being substituted for the pagan holidays? The Romans did celebrate Saturnalia between December 17 and 23, commemorating the winter solstice on December 23, but Christmas does not fit that time frame.

What about the "Birthday of the Unconquered Sun" on December 25? Emperor Aurelian instituted this celebration in AD 274 (therefore, after the Christian celebration of Christmas and perhaps to overshadow the pagan holiday). After legalization in 313, December 25 was purged of any pagan notion. For example, an ancient codex of that time marked December 25 as the "Nativity of the Unconquered" (meaning Jesus), not the "Nativity of the Unconquered Sun." The Emperor Julian (reigned AD 361–363), who had renounced his faith and was therefore known as "the Apostate," wanted to return the empire to paganism. He tried to suppress Christmas by restoring the celebration of the Birth of the Unconquered Sun, a decision reversed upon his death. In sum, Christmas was celebrated on December 25 prior to any pagan celebration on the same date. (See Taylor Marshall, *The Eternal City: Rome and the Origins of Christianity*.)

While we can verify the date of Christmas, the most important point is celebrating the birth of our Lord. Remember *Christmas* is derived from the Old English *Cristes Maesse,* meaning "The Mass of Christ." This Christmas, may we lift up our hearts at the Holy Sacrifice of the Mass and receive our Lord, born again into our souls through the grace of the Holy Eucharist.

The Feast of the Holy Family

On the Sunday between Christmas and New Year's, we traditionally celebrate the feast of the Holy Family. In God's plan of salvation, Jesus entered this time and space in the context of marriage and the family. Although the marriage of St. Joseph and the Blessed Virgin Mary was totally chaste and pure, and although St. Joseph was only the foster and not natural father of Jesus, our Lord lived his early life in a family. His presence, however, elevated the dignity of marriage and the family, and filled the home with his grace.

While the Gospels provide very little information about our Lord's childhood, we can only imagine that the Holy Family must have been much like any family. As a good Jewish husband and father, St. Joseph provided for his family, working as a carpenter. He was the spiritual head of the home, who led his family in prayer each morning and evening, and before meals; who made sure they kept holy the Sabbath; and who brought them to Jerusalem for special holy days, such as Passover. St. Joseph, the good father, provided the strong, masculine example for Jesus. He taught his trade of carpentry to Jesus. Also, according to pious tradition and custom, he taught Jesus to read the Torah.

If St. Joseph was the spiritual head of the home, then surely Blessed Mother Mary was the spiritual heart. As a good Jewish wife and mother, she generously cared for the home, provided the meals, and performed numerous other tasks. As a mother, we can picture Mary holding baby Jesus and singing to him, caring for his bruises and bumps, and telling him stories.

We know Jesus loved and respected his parents very much. After Jesus was found in the Temple, having been separated from his parents, we read how he returned to Nazareth and was obedient to them (see Lk 2:51). Also, in the Gospels, Jesus is known as "the carpenter's son."

Keep in mind that life was not easy for the Holy Family. Taxes were high. They lived under Roman oppression and the political corruption of the Herodians. They suffered from periodic famine and plague.

They also faced normal family issues: suffering, sickness, and death. Consider the anguish St. Joseph and Mary had when they discovered Jesus missing during that visit to Jerusalem. Tradition also holds that St. Joseph died in the presence of Jesus and Mary before the beginning of the public ministry; and then, from the cross, Jesus entrusted his widowed mother to the care of St. John, for there were no siblings to care for her.

In all, Jesus entered the context of marriage and family life, and he sanctified it. He learned from the example of St. Joseph and Blessed Mother Mary. He elevated marriage to a holy sacrament. He showed that a strong marriage and family are founded upon the love of God.

The feast of the Holy Family prompts the faithful to pause and examine their role in the family; parents, in particular, must reflect on their vocation as husband or wife, father or mother. Granted, we live at a time of high divorce. We also live in an age of increasing isolation due to technology. Cell phones and computers increasingly isolate people from others, including their family members. However, if we surrender with a groan of "oh well, that is the way it is," we are doomed.

Therefore, each spouse and parent must first pause, reflect, and reorient his or her life back to our Lord. This reorientation means simply striving to be holy and keeping the priorities of life in proper order—God first, then spouse, then children. Husbands and wives need to pray each day individually and together, and for each other. A husband ought to pray for his wife each day and, looking to the example of St. Joseph, ask, "Am I the best husband I can be? Am I fulfilling my duties to my wife?" On the other hand, a wife ought to pray for her husband each day and, looking to the example of Mary, ask, "Am I the best wife I can be? Am I fulfilling my duties to my husband?

In their hearts, husbands and wives ought to renew their marriage vows at least weekly: "I take you for my husband/wife. I promise to be faithful to you in good times and in bad, in sickness and in health. I will love you and honor you all the days of my life." They should also, through word and deed, show their love and respect for each other, including in the presence of their children. Children will learn how to respect each other, how to respect their future husband or wife, and what to look for in a man or woman when considering marriage by watching how their own parents respect and show their love for each other.

Fathers and mothers ought to pray for each child by name. They need to ask the Holy Spirit for guidance as to how to raise their children, and they must do for each child individually, for, of course, each one is unique. Be mindful of setting a good example in word and deed. A wise professor of mine once said that values are not just taught, they are caught.

Also, families should strive to have a holy family, where Christ is truly the Lord of your home. Pope John Paul II frequently referred to the family as "the domestic church," so create a spiritual environment for your home with crucifixes, statues, and sacred images. When someone comes into a Catholic home, he should immediately know it is a faith-filled home by seeing a crucifix or image of the Sacred Heart of Jesus. A crucifix should be placed over the head of each bed. These are constant reminders of a holy presence, and, in fact, do protect us from evil.

A family ought to strive to live like a holy family by doing the following.

First, **pray together**: say grace before meals and bedtime prayers, whether kneeling down with the little ones or reminding the big ones. Read Sacred Scripture together. And pray the Rosary together (even if it is just a decade when little ones are fidgety). Of course, Sunday Mass is essential. If parents will not give Almighty God due worship, how can they expect children to respect and obey them? Occasionally when I have been to homes for dinner, I have been invited to join in family prayers. I remember once kneeling with the family around the parents' bed and praying the Our Father, Hail Mary, and Glory Be; having each person be thankful for something during the day; and finally having a litany of "God bless so and so." I have always thought this a wonderful way to end the day. Someone may have had a miserable day at work or school, or have had a disagreement with someone—even a family member—but now, as a family, they are praying together with our Lord. I have also known parents who will kneel at the crib of their newborn child and say family prayers. Again, as Pope St. John Paul II wisely said, "Families that pray together stay together."

Another important aspect of prayer is taking time for regular sacramental confession. I suggest a monthly confession. Here family members are recognizing their sins—many of which are probably committed against each other—and then seek forgiveness. The sacrament of Penance not only forgives and heals but also strengthens a person to do better and avoid occasions of sin. Also, if a person recognizes his own failings and seeks forgiveness from the Lord, he is more likely to seek forgiveness directly from those he had hurt. Think of how many family relationships would be strengthened and benefited by hearing one member say to another, "I am sorry. Please forgive me."

Prayer cannot be over-emphasized. Several studies related to the practice of prayer, church attendance, and the practice of natural family planning have found that while there is a tragic 50 percent divorce rate in the United States in the first five years of marriage, the divorce rate drops to 10 percent if a couple and a family attend church each Sunday. And if they pray together each day, to 5 percent; and if they do not contracept, 1 percent. What— or who—makes the difference? God.

Second, **teach your children the Faith.** Help them know the Faith. A family cannot rely on a Catholic school or religious education program alone, no matter how good those programs may be. Talk to them about the moral issues and what we believe as Catholics. We are not called to be like everyone else; we are called to be Christians and members of the Catholic Church. Parents must instill a Catholic Christian identity in their children from the beginning of their lives. Regular education may prepare a child for a successful future in this life; religious education prepares a child for a life with the Lord now and for the future with him in heaven.

Third, **remind children about sin and its consequences.** I always had a healthy fear of committing a mortal sin and the punishment of hell. I did not want to end up in hell. And I have to admit that, at times, this healthy fear kept me from making some bad decisions. King St. Louis IX of France (d. 1270) wrote to his son, "My first instruction is that you should love the Lord your God with all your heart and all your strength. . . . You should permit yourself to be tormented by every kind of martyrdom before you would allow yourself to commit a mortal sin" (from the *Liturgy of the Hours* for the feast of St. Louis, August 25).

Fourth, **talk with your children.** Dinnertime is important. Strive to have dinner, or at least one meal a day, as a family. With busy schedules, having a family dinner presents a real challenge, so strategize. I have a friend who owns a restaurant and is also the main chef, which prevents him from being at home for dinner most evenings. So he and his family have breakfast together, and when he comes home, desert. On weekends, the family joins him at his restaurant. However, on Sunday morning, after Mass, he and the family have a brunch together, which everyone helps prepare. The benefits to the family meal together are real. The University of Michigan found that among families that eat together four times a week, there is a significant drop in divorce, high school drop-out, drug and alcohol abuse, and teenage pregnancy. Dinnertime also is a good time to pray, talk about the Faith, and know what is happening in each other's lives. Therefore, make time for the family dinner, put away the technology, and seize the opportunity to share life as a family.

Fifth, **revere the father**. Fathers are absent in our country, due to either divorce or long work hours. A friend who teaches religion in a Catholic high school told me that one time, when speaking of fatherhood, he had his students write down the qualities they see in their fathers. Noticing that one student had finished quickly, he went over to her desk, looked at the paper, and saw one word: *absent*.

The media mocks fathers, presenting him as the family dummy. Yet fathers are important. Even the heavenly Father knew Jesus needed St. Joseph. Jesus and the Blessed Mother loved and revered him. Fathers, however, need to do their job. Religion should not just be delegated to Mom. The idea that "dads coach and moms pray" is nonsense. Children, especially sons, need to see fathers on their knees praying and praying with them. They need to have their fathers devoutly worshipping at Mass and going to confession. A Swiss study found that if fathers attend church regularly, even without the mothers, 75 percent of children will become regular church goers. Fathers are essential.

Therefore, on the feast of the Holy Family, take time to reflect on your family and your role in particular. Family life will always be a struggle. When the love of God is present, when each member is mindful that he or she is a child of God, when each strives to live in that love and work for the salvation of others, then a family is strong. With the presence of Christ in our hearts and our home, and with the prayers and example of St. Joseph and our Blessed Mother to help us, our family will stay on the right path and find salvation.

The Solemnity of Mary, Mother of God, January 1

On January 1, the eighth day of the Octave of Christmas, the Church celebrates Mary under the title "Mother of God." To understand this title, we must first clearly understand Mary's role as mother of our Savior, Jesus Christ. As Catholics, we firmly believe in the incarnation of our Lord. Mary conceived by the power of the Holy Spirit (see Lk 1:26–38; Mt 1:18–25). Through her, Jesus Christ entered this world, taking on human flesh and a human soul. As we profess in the Nicene Creed, "for us men and for our salvation, he came down from heaven, and by the Holy Spirit was incarnate of the Virgin Mary, and became man."

Jesus is true God and true man. In his divine person are united both a divine nature and a human nature, which is called the hypostatic union. Mary did not create the divine person of Jesus, who existed with the Father and Holy Spirit from all eternity. In fact, "the One whom she conceived as man by the Holy Spirit, who truly became her Son according to the flesh, was none other than the Father's eternal Son, the second person of the Holy Trinity. Hence the Church confesses that Mary is truly 'Mother of God' (*Theotokos*)" (CCC 495).

Sometime in the early history of the Church, our Blessed Mother was given the title "Mother of God." St. John Chrysostom (d. 407), for example, composed in his Eucharistic Prayer for the Mass an anthem in honor of her: "It is truly just to proclaim you blessed, O Mother of God, who are most blessed, all pure and Mother of our God. We magnify you who are more honorable than the Cherubim and incomparably more glorious than the Seraphim. You who, without losing your virginity, gave birth to the Word of God. You who are truly the Mother of God."

However, objection to the title "Mother of God" arose in the fifth century due to confusion over the mystery of the Incarnation. Nestorius, Bishop of Constantinople (428–431), incited a major controversy. He stated that Mary gave birth to Jesus Christ, a regular human person, *period*. To this human person was united the person of the Word of God (the divine Jesus). This union of two persons—the human Christ and the divine Word—was "sublime and unique" but merely accidental. The divine person dwelt in the human person "as in a temple." Following his own reasoning, Nestorius asserted that the human Jesus died on the cross, not the divine Jesus. As such, Mary is not "Mother of God," but simply "Mother of Christ"—the human Jesus. Sound confusing? It is, but the result is the splitting of Christ into two persons, and thereby the denial of the Incarnation and ultimately the denial of redemption.

St. Cyril, Bishop of Alexandria (d. 440), refuted Nestorius, asserting, 'It was not that an ordinary man was born first of the Holy Virgin, on whom afterwards the Word descended; what we say is that, being united with the flesh from the womb, [the Word] has undergone birth in the flesh, making the birth in the flesh His own."

On June 22, 431, the Council of Ephesus convened to settle this argument. The council declared, "If anyone does not confess that the Emmanuel is truly God and therefore that the holy Virgin is the Mother of God (*Theotokos*) (since she begot according to the flesh the Word of God made flesh), *anathema sit*." Therefore, the council officially recognized that Jesus is one divine person, with two natures—human and divine—united in a true union. Second, the Council of Ephesus affirmed that our Blessed Mother could rightfully be called the Mother of God. Mary is not Mother of God the Father, or Mother of God the Holy Spirit; rather, she is Mother of God, the Son—Jesus Christ, true God from all eternity who entered this world becoming also true man. The Council of Ephesus declared Nestorius a heretic, and the Emperor Theodosius ordered him deposed and exiled. (Interestingly, a small Nestorian Church still exists in Iraq, Iran, and Syria.)

The Incarnation is indeed a profound mystery. The Church uses very precise—albeit philosophical—language to prevent confusion and error. Since we have just celebrated Christmas and now celebrate the Solemnity of Mary, Mother of God, we must continue to ponder this great mystery of how our divine Savior entered this world, taking on our human flesh, to free us from sin. We must also ponder and emulate the great example of our Blessed Mother, who said, "I am the handmaid of the Lord; be it done unto me according to thy word."

A Meditation

Let us not forget that Mary is truly "mother." She is not just the physical means by which our Lord entered this world, but she is also in the fullest sense *mother* and our mother in the life of grace. As mother, she always wants to present her Son to others and to lead others to her divine Son. In the Gospels, she presented him to the shepherds, the magi, and the priest Simeon and Anna. She interceded for the wedding party at Cana. She desires to do the same for each of us. When our Lord died on the cross, standing there were his mother, Mary, and St. John the Apostle; Jesus said to Mary, "Woman, there is your son," entrusting his widowed mother to the care of St. John; and to St. John, "Here is your mother" (see Jn 19:26–27). Traditionally, we have always held that here Jesus gave Mary as a mother to the Church as a whole and to each of us.

This belief is beautifully illustrated in the message of our Blessed Mother at Guadalupe, when she appeared to St. Juan Diego in 1531. On December 9, she said, "Know for certain, least of my sons, that I am the perfect and perpetual Virgin Mary, Mother of Jesus, the true God. . . . I am your merciful mother, the merciful mother of all of you who live united in this land, and of all mankind, of all those who love me, of those who cry to me, of those who seek me, and of those who have confidence in me. Here I will hear their weeping, their sorrow, and will remedy and alleviate all their multiple sufferings, necessities, and misfortunes."

As we celebrate a new year of our Lord, Anno Domini, let us look to our Blessed Mother's example and rely on her prayers. Say the Rosary and ponder the mysteries of our Lord's life through the eyes of Mary. May we turn to her always as our own Mother, pleading, "Holy Mary, Mother of God, pray for us sinners now and at the hour of our death. Amen."

The Feast of the Holy Name
of Jesus, January 3

When the angel appeared to St. Joseph in a dream, he said, "Joseph, son of David, do not be afraid to take Mary your wife into your home. For it is through the Holy Spirit that this child was conceived in her. She will bear a son and you are to name him Jesus, because he will save his people from their sins" (Mt 1:21). (The name *Jesus* means, "Yahweh saves.")

What is most important is that each of us shows proper respect, reverence, and devotion for the holy name of Jesus. St. Paul, in his letter to the Philippians, wrote, "At the name of Jesus every knee should bend of those in heaven and on earth and under the earth, and every tongue confess that Jesus Christ is Lord, to the glory of God the Father" (2:10–11). Just as a name gives identity to a person, the holy name of Jesus reminds the hearer of who he is and what he has done for us. Keep in mind that the name *Jesus* means "Yahweh saves" or "Yahweh is salvation."

In invoking our Lord's name with reverential faith, one is turning to him and imploring his divine assistance. An old spiritual manual cited four special rewards of invoking the Holy Name. First, the name of Jesus brings help in bodily needs. At the Ascension, Jesus himself promised that much and more (see Mk 16:17–19).

Second, the name of Jesus gives help in spiritual trials. Jesus forgave sins, and through the invocation of his Holy Name, sins continue to be forgiven. At Pentecost, St. Peter echoed the prophecy of Joel that "everyone shall be saved who calls on the name of the Lord" (Acts 2:21). As St. Stephen, the first martyr, was being stoned, he called upon the name of the Lord and prayed, "Lord Jesus, receive my spirit" (Acts 7:59).

Third, the name of Jesus protects the person against Satan and his temptations. Jesus, on his own authority, rebuked Satan and exorcized demons (e.g., the temptations in the desert; see Mt 4:1–11).

Finally, we receive every grace and blessing through the Holy Name of Jesus. He said, "Amen, amen, I say to you, whatever you ask the Father in my name, he will give you" (Jn 16:23–24). In summary, St. Paul said that whatever we do, in word or deed, we should do it in the name of Jesus" (see Col 3:17).

Sadly, too many Christians use the name of Jesus irreverently, not only in anger, but also as a mere expletive. A few years ago, I was in a small store and the radio was broadcasting some sports show with the announcer recapping the Redskins game; I was shocked to hear the announcer use the holy name of Jesus when talking about a botched Redskins play. I can only think how Satan must delight when he hears people blaspheme in such ways and commit mortal sin. I also thought, "If a person were in Saudi Arabia and he blasphemed the name of Mohammed, a mere mortal, he would have his head cut off."

The *Catechism* teaches, "Blasphemy is directly opposed to the second commandment. It consists in uttering against God—inwardly or outwardly—words of hatred, reproach, or defiance; in speaking ill of God; in failing in respect toward Him in one's speech; in misusing God's name. . . . Blasphemy is contrary to the respect due God and His holy name. It is in itself a grave sin" (2148).

For good reason, the popes over the centuries have encouraged due reverence. In 1597, Pope Sixtus V granted an indulgence to anyone reverently saying, "Praised be Jesus Christ!" Pope Clement VII in 1530 allowed a feast day in honor of the Holy Name, which Pope Innocent XIII extended to the universal Church in 1721; although this feast day was dropped in 1969 in the revision of the liturgical calendar, Pope St. John Paul II reinstituted it to be celebrated on January 3. Pope Pius IX in 1862 approved a Litany of the Holy Name of Jesus, which Pope Leo XIII later endorsed for the whole Church because he was "desirous of seeing an increase in the devotion toward this glorious name of Jesus among the faithful, especially in a period when this august name is shamelessly scoffed at."

May each of us respect the holy name of Jesus and admonish those who do not. When we hear someone take the Lord's name in vain, consider doing the following: (1) bow the head; (2) pray for the Lord to forgive him, even audibly saying, "Lord, forgive him"; and (3) say, "Please, don't blaspheme."

IHS & XP

IHS is a Christogram (a combination of letters) which represents the holy name *Jesus*. Early scribes would abbreviate the sacred names of Jesus by using the first two letters of the name, or the first and last letters, with a line over the letters. I (Iota) and H (Eta) are the first two Greek letters for "Jesus." Sometime in the second century, the third letter, S (Sigma), was added, thereby rendering IHS. Also, the letters X and P represent the first two Greek letters, X (Chi) and P (Rho), for the word *Christos*; that is, Christ.

These Christograms, such as XP or IHS, served as secret codes during the Roman persecution. Inscribed on a tomb, they indicated a deceased Christian, or inscribed on a doorpost, a Christian home.

St. Bernardine of Siena (1380–1444) and his student St. John of Capistrano (1386–1456) used the Christogram IHS to promote devotion to the Holy Name of Jesus. In their preaching missions throughout Italy, they carried wooden placards with the IHS surrounded by rays. St. Bernardine and St. John blessed the faithful with this Christogram, invoking the Holy Name of Jesus, and many miracles were reported. They also encouraged people to have the Christogram placed over the city gates and the doorways of their homes, instead of a family crest, to show their devotion and allegiance to the Lord. Countering the objections of some who considered this veneration superstitious, Pope Martin V in 1427 approved the proper veneration to the Holy Name and asked that the cross be included in the monogram IHS. Largely due to St. Bernadine's preaching, the name *Jesus* was added to the Hail Mary, "blessed is the fruit of thy womb, Jesus."

During this time also, because of the decline of Greek and predominance of Latin, IHS was viewed as an acronym for the Latin *Iesus Hominum Salvator*, meaning "Jesus Savior of Mankind."

The Epiphany, January 6

January 6 marks the feast of the Epiphany, the Twelfth Day of Christmas. (In the United States, the Epiphany is celebrated on the Sunday after January 1, the Solemnity of Mary Mother of God.) The Epiphany commemorates the awakening of the whole world—Jew and Gentile—to the presence of the newborn Savior. Three important aspects of the Gospel account deserve attention: the star, the magi, and King Herod.

The Star of Bethlehem

The magi from the East said to King Herod, "Where is the new-born King of the Jews? We saw his star at its rising and have come to do him homage" (Mt 2:2).

What was this star? The answer lies not only in the scientific evidence but the spiritual significance of that evidence. Let's begin with the scientific evidence. Over the years, several findings have been presented to identify the star. Keep in mind that any dating is problematic due to variations in calendars (Julian v. Hebrew v.

Gregorian) and record keeping. Nevertheless, some possibilities include the following. First, around 10 BC, Halley's comet was visible (although it was not named after Halley at the time); however, since comets usually indicated doom and disaster, this does not seem to be a good contender.

Second, Johannes Kepler (d. 1630), who wrote the *Laws of Planetary Motion*, proposed that the conjunction of the planets Jupiter, Saturn, and Mars caused a brilliant light (about 7 BC). Kepler had observed such a phenomenon in 1604 and calculated that this would have occurred at about the time of Christ's birth. He posited that a supernova occurred simultaneously which would have caused an intense, brilliant light lasting for weeks.

Third, the Austrian astronomer Konradin Ferrari d'Occhieppo in 2003 proposed that the star was the conjunction of Saturn and Jupiter in the constellation Pisces in 7–6 BC. He wrote, "Jupiter, the star of the highest Babylonian deity [Marduke], entered its brightest phase when it rose in the evening alongside Saturn, the cosmic representation of the Jewish people." He then posited that astronomers in Babylon (an ancient center for astronomy) would have interpreted this phenomenon as a universally significant event; namely, the birth of a king in the land of the Jews who would bring salvation. I think the constellation Pisces has significance since Pisces represents "fish" and our Lord said to the apostles that he would make them fishers of men (see Mt 4:19). (D'Occhieppo's work was cited by Pope Benedict XVI in his book *Jesus of Nazareth*, volume I, pp. 97–102.)

Finally, Roger Sinnott, an astronomer, using evidence from Bryant Tuckeman's book *Planetary, Lunar, and Solar Positions, 601 BC to AD 1* (1962), presented a most interesting finding. In 3 or 2 BC, three unusual planetary alignments (a triple conjunction) of the planets Jupiter and Venus with the star Regulus in the constellation Leo occurred. The splendor of this event would have climaxed on December 25, 2 BC. Jupiter was named for Jupiter, the king of the Roman gods; Venus, named for Venus, the Roman goddess of love and motherhood; Regulus, a star which means "little king" and symbolizes a scepter; and Leo, the lion, the symbol for the tribe of Judah. One could suggest that here was a symbolic revelation of the Father (the King) sending his Son (the little King) into this world through Mary (the mother) to the land of Judah (the lion), the people of the covenant. Remember, too, we read in Genesis 49:9–10: "Judah, like a lion's whelp, you have grown up on prey, my son. He crouches like the lion recumbent, the king of beasts—who would dare rouse him? The scepter shall never depart from Judah, or the mace from between his legs." Sinnott posited that the magi would have easily interpreted this event as a sign of the birth of the Messiah. Astrophysicists also cite such an alignment occurs about every thirty-eight thousand years. Perhaps this explanation is the best.

Archeologists have also found evidence of some unique star being observed at the time of our Lord's birth. Egyptian records (5–2 BC) indicate that in the month Mesori, the star Sirius, the dog star, rose at sunrise with extraordinary brilliance. Mesori means "the birth of a prince," and the Egyptian astrologers interpreted this event to mean "the birth of a new king into this world." Chinese records show that about 4 BC, a brilliant star appeared in the sky for a long time.

The Jewish prophecies also pointed to a star that would announce the birth of the Messiah: "A star [*anatole*, "rising star"] shall come forth out of Jacob, and a scepter shall rise out of Israel" (Nm 24:17).

Whatever the "star" actually was, Almighty God used this phenomenon to announce the birth of his Son, our Divine Messiah and Savior. Moreover, he used it to excite the magi, the Gentiles, to come searching. In sum, St. Gregory Nazianzen said, "The very moment when the Magi, guided by the star, adored Christ the new king, astrology came to an end, because the stars were now moving in the orbit determined by Christ." As we continue our Christmas celebration, may we, too, orient our lives—spiritually, emotionally, economically, politically, socially, and in a word, totally—to Jesus. May we follow the true Light that penetrates the darkness and allow his light to shine forth in our own lives.

The Magi

The Gospel of Matthew mentions the magi who came from the East to worship the newborn Christ child (see Mt 2:1–12). Exactly who the magi were though remains somewhat of a mystery.

Oftentimes, the English translations of the Bible use the word *astrologers* for magi. In the original Greek text, the word *magos* (*magoi*, plural) has four meanings: (1) a member of the priestly class of ancient Persia, where astrology and astronomy were prominent in biblical times, a fact to which the ancient historian Herodotus (d. fifth century BC) attested; (2) one who had occult knowledge and power, and was adept at dream interpretation, astrology, fortune-telling, divination, and spiritual mediation; (3) a magician; or (4) a charlatan, who preyed upon people using the before mentioned practices.

From these possible definitions and the description provided in the Gospel, the magi were probably priest-astrologers who could interpret the stars, particularly the significance of the star that proclaimed the birth of the Messiah. They probably came from the area of Babylon (present Iraq, but then an area controlled by Persia), where astrology was popular and the world-famous

observatory of Sippar existed. Archeologists have found cuneiform tablets where the observatory existed that speak of the observed star. Moreover, they probably also knew the prophecy concerning the Jewish Messiah, since during the Jewish exile, the prophet Daniel was King Nebuchadnezzar's chief *magos*. Also, according the historian Giulio Firpo, being under Persian control (if not Persians themselves), they would have known the Zoroastrian tradition that "the prince of virtue will triumph over evil thanks to the benefactor, truth incarnate, who is to be born of a virgin, to whom no man will come close," and who will deliver justice to mankind and resurrect the dead (*Three Kings, Ten Mysteries*, pp. 71–72).

More importantly, the visit of the magi fulfilled the prophecies of the Old Testament: Balaam prophesied about the coming Messiah marked by a star: "I see him, though not now; I behold him, though not near: A star shall advance from Jacob and a staff shall rise from Israel" (Nm 24:17). Psalm 72 speaks of how the Gentiles will come to worship the Messiah: "The kings of Tarshish and the Isles shall offer gifts, / the kings of Arabia and Seba shall bring tribute. / All kings shall pay him homage, / all nations shall serve him" (Ps 72:10–11). Isaiah also prophesied the gifts. "Caravans of camels shall fill you, dromedaries from Midian and Ephah; all from Sheba shall come bearing gold and frankincense, and proclaiming the praises of the Lord" (Is 60:6).

St. Matthew recorded that the magi brought three gifts: gold, frankincense, and myrrh. Each gift had a prophetic meaning: gold, the gift for a king; frankincense, the gift for a priest; and myrrh (a burial ointment), a gift for one who would die. St. Irenaeus (d. 202), in his *Adversus haereses*, offered the following interpretation for the gifts of gold, frankincense, and myrrh respectively: King, God, and Suffering Redeemer, as well as virtue, prayer, and suffering.

The earliest tradition is inconsistent as to the number of the magi. The Eastern tradition favored twelve magi. In the West, several of the early Church fathers—including Origen, St. Leo the Great, and St. Maximus of Turin—accepted three magi. Early Christian paintings in Rome found at the cemetery of Sts. Peter and Marcellinus depict two magi, and at the cemetery of St. Domitilla, four.

Nevertheless, traditionally, we do think of the three magi as "the three kings." We usually have the three kings in our nativity sets. We even sing, "We three kings of orient are." Here the three gifts, Psalm 72, and the rising star in the East, converge to render the magi as three kings traveling from the East.

Since the seventh century in the Western Church, the magi have been identified as Caspar (sometimes spelled *Gaspar*), Melchior, and Balthasar. A work called the *Excerpta et Collectanea* attributed to St. Bede (d. 735) wrote that "the magi were the ones who gave gifts to the Lord. The first is said to have been Melchior, an old man with white hair and a long beard . . . who offered gold to the Lord as to a king. The second, Caspar by name, young and beardless and ruddy complexioned . . . honored Him as God by his gift of incense, an oblation worthy of divinity. The third, black-skinned and heavily bearded, named Balthasar . . . by his gift of myrrh testified to the Son of Man who was to die." An excerpt from a medieval calendar of saints printed in Cologne read, "Having undergone many trials and fatigues for the Gospel, the three wise men met at Sewa (Sebaste in Armenia) in the year 54 to celebrate the feast of Christmas. Thereupon, after the celebration of Mass, they died: St. Melchior on January 1, aged 116; St. Balthasar on January 6th, aged 112; and St. Caspar on January 11th, aged 109." The Roman Martyrology also lists these dates as the magi's respective feast days.

Emperor Zeno brought the relics of the magi from Persia to Constantinople in 490. Relics (whether the same or others) appeared in Milan much later and were kept at the Basilica of St. Eustorgius. Emperor Frederick Barbarossa of Germany, who plundered Italy, took the relics to Cologne in 1162, where they remain secure to this day in a beautiful reliquary housed in the cathedral.

Even though some mystery remains to the identity of the magi, the Church respects their act of worship. The Council of Trent, when underscoring the reverence that must be given to the Holy Eucharist, decreed, "The faithful of Christ venerate this most holy sacrament with the worship of *latria* which is due to the true God. . . . For in this sacrament we believe that the same God is present whom the eternal Father brought into the world, saying of Him, 'Let all God's angels worship Him.' It is the same God whom the Magi fell down and worshiped, and finally, the same God whom the apostles adored in Galilee as Scripture says" (*Decree on the Most Holy Eucharist*, 5).

Having celebrated Christmas and the feast of the Epiphany, we too must be mindful of our duty to adore our Lord through prayer, worship, and self-sacrificing good works. St. Gregory Nazianzen (d. 389) preached, "Let us remain on in adoration; and to Him, who, in order to save us, humbled Himself to such a degree of poverty as to receive our body, let us offer not only incense, gold and myrrh . . . but also spiritual gifts, more sublime than those which can be seen with the eyes" (*Oratio*, 19).

King Herod, Priests, and Scribes

The Epiphany account in the Gospel warns the faithful to be on guard against evil (see Mt 2). Evil attacks in various ways. The first attack is indirect—apathy. When the magi arrived, King Herod consulted the priests and scribes who quoted the prophecies. One would have thought they would have been thrilled to know that at last the prophecies had been fulfilled and the Messiah had been born. They should have rushed to go and see the Lord. They did not. They recited what the Scriptures said and then stayed home. Such is the evil of apathy!

The second attack is direct—plotting, befriending, scheming, manipulating, but all to destroy. King Herod was an evil man. He was the puppet ruler of Judea, appointed by Caesar Augustus in the year 40 BC. He sold his soul and body literally to be king. Upon his appointment, he offered sacrifice to the god Jupiter in Rome—think, a Jew offering pagan sacrifice! He did keep peace between Rome and the Jewish people, albeit sometimes using ruthless tactics to squelch any disturbance.

He was also a suspicious and paranoid man. He guarded his power and quickly eliminated any threat to it. He murdered his own wife, three of his sons, and mother-in-law because he thought they were plotting against him. Caesar Augustus said that "it was safer to be Herod's pig than his son," a play on the Greek words *hus*, pig, and *huios*, son. Do not forget, he lied to the magi, asking them to inform him where Jesus, the newborn king, was, so he too could worship him; his true intent was to kill baby Jesus. When the magi left by a different route and did not report back to him, he ordered the slaughter of the Holy Innocents, boys two years old and younger.

When he reached the age of seventy and knew death was imminent, Herod retired to his palace in Jericho and ordered three hundred of the most prominent, wealthy, and influential people arrested on trumped-up charges and imprisoned. The plan was that, upon his death, they would be taken to the Hippodrome and slaughtered so that at least someone would shed some tears when he died. Archeologists conclude that Herod died from some kind of cancer that ate him from the inside out; spiritually, one could opine that the cancer in question was sin.

A Meditation

On this feast of the Epiphany, we again set our sights on the star of Christ. We offer daily the same gifts: gold, frankincense, and myrrh. First, we need to bring a gift of gold, the gift for a king. Gold is a beautiful, pure element. Our faith must be that very way: pure and simple. We cannot have a conditional faith, as in "if you do this, God, I will do that"; nor an *a la carte* faith, as in "I'll pick this teaching and that, stir it all together and still call myself a Catholic"; nor a lax faith, as in "Jesus loves me just the way I am so I don't have to go to Mass, confess my sins, or work on my faults," or "I visit Jesus at Christmas and Easter, for baptisms, marriages, and funerals—that is good enough." No, faith must be constantly refined to become like pure gold. We need to recognize with this gift that Jesus is truly our king, on every level, and every aspect of our life. As such, we must conform our lives to the Word of God, not conform the Word of God to fit our lives.

Second, we need to bring Jesus the gift of frankincense, recognizing him as our priest. Though the word *priest* comes from the Latin *presbyter*, one of the titles for the pope, pontiff, derives from *pontifex*, which means "bridge builder." Jesus built a bridge between God and mankind. We therefore look to Jesus to find the Father. Jesus said, "Whoever has seen me has seen the Father" (Jn 15:9). We unite ourselves to Christ, and thereby the Father in union with the Holy Spirit, through our daily prayer and worship. We share his divine life through the Holy Eucharist. We receive his forgiveness in the sacrament of Penance. We grow in our knowledge by our study of the Faith, especially Sacred Scripture. In so doing, Christ, the priest, one day will present us to the heavenly Father.

Finally, we need to bring the gift of myrrh to Jesus, recognizing that he suffered and died for us. He as Priest took the burden of sin—our sins—onto himself and offered himself on the altar of the cross as the perfect sacrifice to reconcile us to the Father. We should never lose sight of that cross. We too suffer, whether bearing physical problems, family problems, or work problems. We all suffer. Each day we need to put that suffering in a coffer, as did the kings, and offer it to Jesus to atone for our sins, the sins of others, the sins of the souls in purgatory. We stand with Jesus at the cross never losing sight of the resurrection. Yes, we bring these gifts each day. By doing so, we will be awake to Jesus.

We must be careful however. Evil lurks. The priests and scribes still lurk. Their apathy can be contagious. How hard it is to be faithful and good when others, especially our loved ones, are apathetic! The faithful and good person could easily succumb and say, "Why bother? Who cares?"

Herod still lurks. There are the new Herods who would seek to destroy the presence of Christ. They tempt us to sin. They give us all the excuses and rationalizations like, "Oh, come do this, no one will know. Oh, the Church is outdated, no one believes that anymore. Oh, I'll be your friend if you fudge the accounts, cheat on the test, or sleep with me. Oh, you'll be a rising star in the political party if your abandon your Christian principles." They offer us friendship, popularity, position, and power. They tempt us to build our own little kingdom now and forget about the kingdom of God. In the end, they seek to destroy Christ and us too. Remember, King Herod died, lost his kingdom, and faced judgment. If it were not for the Gospels, he would be long-forgotten; but what a way to be remembered!

We need to live the Epiphany. We need to be awake to our Lord each day, present our gifts to him, and follow his light. Then one day, by his grace, we will come into his perfect presence in heaven.

An Epiphany Custom

For centuries, Catholics in Austria, Germany, and Switzerland have marked the Epiphany with a special custom. The parish priest will visit a house and mark the lintel of the front door with chalk with an inscription—for example, 20*C+M+B+19, which signifies 2019 for the year; C for Caspar, M for Melchior, and B for Balthasar; a star (*) for the star that guided the magi; and three crosses for the Holy Trinity. Many also suggest that the C+M+B signifies *Christus mansionem benedicat*, meaning "May Christ bless this house."

Also, there is the *Sternsinger* custom. On this day, children and teenagers will dress as the magi and walk through the neighborhood, led by a child carrying a star. They sing carols and stop at homes just as the magi came to visit baby Jesus. Here they collect money or other items for the poor.

Looking at this custom, if a priest is not available, the father of the family could easily make the inscription on the lintel of the front door of the home. Based on the Collect for the Mass of the Epiphany of the Roman Missal, a simple prayer might be as follows:

O God, who on this day revealed your Only Begotten Son to the nations by the guidance of the star, grant that his presence may dwell in this home and protect them from the darkness of all evil. May the light of faith brighten their lives, and guide their daily activities. May they live in peace and harmony as did the Holy Family. May they be generous with their time, talent, and treasure in responding to the needs of others. And having kept the Faith, may they be brought to behold the beauty of your glory in heaven.

An Epiphany celebration could be held, whereby neighbors could enjoy some refreshment and bring a donation for the poor. Also, the parish youth group could organize a similar *Sternsinger*, going to neighborhoods to collect food or money for a charitable cause.

The Baptism of the Lord

The Epiphany celebrated the awakening of the world to Jesus, the Word of God who became flesh. Yes, the world had been awakened to the Lord and Savior, the Messiah who had come to save both Jew and Gentile, the righteous and the sinner.

Now we celebrate another Epiphany, another awakening; that is, the Baptism of the Lord. Thirty years have passed. Jesus is ready to step from the shadows of his hidden life in Nazareth and into the spotlight of his public ministry. St. John the Baptist, our Lord's cousin and the last great prophet, had been preparing the way. He preached repentance and conversion, baptizing to show a cleansing of sin and start of a new life. Keep in mind that John's baptism was a ritual washing, symbolizing purification; ours is a sacramental baptism intrinsically connected with the passion, death, and resurrection of our Lord. This is why John said, "He will baptize you with the Holy Spirit and fire" (Lk 3:16).

Keep in mind that Jesus is free of all sin; he did not need to be baptized. However, consider what happened when Jesus was baptized: the heavens opened, the Holy Spirit descended as a dove, and the voice of the Father said, "This is my beloved Son." Here is another epiphany, an awakening of the world to the explicit revelation of the Holy Trinity, Father, Son, and Holy Spirit. Here the heavenly Father presented to the world the Lord, Savior, Messiah. Just as a dove appeared at the time of Noah after the flood washed away evil and renewed creation, here the Holy Spirit in the form of a dove showed a new order of grace, a new kingdom, and a new covenant. Here also is a foreshadowing of the saving act of our Lord. As Jesus is immersed in the depths of the water and then rises, we foresee Jesus plunged in the depths of sin and death itself, but rising, conquering sin and death, opening the gates of heaven and giving new life, where we will behold the face of God, Father, Son, and Holy Spirit in the beatific vision. Another interesting point is the phrasing "the heavens opened." In the original Greek text, the verb is *schizo*, meaning "to rip" or "to tear." The heavens are torn open to show God's decisive interaction in this world, and when our Lord dies on the cross, the Temple veil is ripped open to show the old covenant, the old order, has passed away; God's saving action has made the new perfect covenant, a new creation.

As we ponder this scene, we must recall our own baptism. The saving mystery lives on and is shared with us through the sacrament of Baptism. Jesus told the apostles at the ascension, "Go out, preach the Gospel, teach everything I have commanded you, make disciples, and baptize in the name of the Trinity" (cf. Mt 28:18–20). When each of us was baptized by the pouring of water and the invocation of the Holy Trinity, original sin and all sin was washed away. Sanctifying grace—that sharing in the divine nature of God and in his life and love—was infused into our souls. Sanctifying grace elevates our nature to something even greater than that given to Adam and Eve at creation. Just as Jesus humbled himself to share in our humanity, we share in his divinity through sanctifying grace. Rightly, we can refer to the Father as "Father" and to Jesus as "Lord, Savior, and Brother." The Holy Spirit sealed our soul with a character by which a person can say, "I am a child of God, a Christian, and a member of the Catholic Church, the Church Jesus founded." Moreover, to live this baptism, the Spirit empowers us with the supernatural virtues of faith, hope, and love, with the graced moral virtues of prudence, justice, fortitude, and temperance, and with his seven-fold gifts (which will be fulfilled at Confirmation).

In all, with baptism, we begin a life journey. As the Lord spoke through Isaiah and said, "I will take you by the hand" (Is 41:13), so Jesus extends his hand to grasp ours. He leads us like the Good Shepherd through the good times of verdant pasture when we rejoice, through the tough times of dark valleys. Of course, this baptismal grace and character are strengthened through Holy Communion and Confirmation. Note that St. John taught, "Three testify water, blood and the Spirit": water for Baptism, blood for Holy Eucharist, and spirit for Confirmation. These three sacraments of initiation complete our membership in the Church (see 1 Jn 5:6–7). Although not technically a sacrament of initiation, Penance restores the grace weakened, even lost, due to sin. As we journey with our Lord, sharing our life with him through prayer, worship, good work, and the study of the Faith, this baptismal character becomes stronger, and the sanctifying grace more magnetic, moving us to say not only, "I believe," but also, "I want to believe more. I want to love you more." One day, we hope to see our baptism and the life of grace fulfilled when our Lord leads us safely through the gates of heaven and presents us to his Father. What a beautiful gift!

While we have been awakened, we must also make Christ manifest in our lives. Pope Benedict taught, "Baptism commits

Christians to participate boldly in the spread of the Kingdom of God, cooperating if necessary with the sacrifice of one's own life. Certainly, not everyone is called to a bloody martyrdom. There is also an unbloody martyrdom, which is no less significant. It is the silent and heroic testimony of many Christians who live the Gospel without compromises, fulfilling their duty and dedicating themselves generously in service to the poor."

In the world in which we live, we must be witnesses. Never should we forget that many of our brothers and sisters in Christ do bear the ultimate witness; over one hundred thousand Christians die each year due to religious persecution, especially in Islamic countries. In recent years, when the ISIS murderers took the town of Mosul, they gathered fifteen children and said, "Convert or die." Each child replied, "We love Jesus. We will not convert." They all were martyred for the Faith. I can only imagine that the heavens were torn open, that God said, "These are my beloved children," and welcomed them to heaven.

What great faith! Ours, however, may be an unbloody martyrdom. For there are many people who consider religion—especially Christianity—and the Church as the enemy. Nevertheless, we speak and live by truth rather than live by political correctness. We do not idolize things of this world—money, material goods, power, honors, position—but worship God and use such things for his glory, our good, and the good of others. We do not waste our lives on passing sensual pleasures but invest our lives in the things of God. We do not seek a passing joy that leaves us spent and empty, but a greater joy that fulfills and increases. Such witness of God's truth and love brings justice and peace. Such witness also makes converts.

On this solemnity, let us rejoice and celebrate. Everyone should know his or her own date of baptism and celebrate that day each day like a spiritual birthday. For example, St. Louis IX, King of France (d. 1270), signed his name, "Louis of Poissy." Usually, kings would sign, "Louis of Rheims," because that was the cathedral in which they were crowned. One day, a nobleman asked, "Your majesty, why do you sign 'Louis of Poissy' instead of 'Louis of Rheims'?" St. Louis replied, "In Rheims, I was crowned king, but in Poissy I was baptized and became a child of God and a member of his Church."

A Spiritual Opportunity

To celebrate the Baptism of the Lord, the family could gather for dinner or the main meal of the day. Each person of the family could read his or her baptismal certificate out loud to the others, and then they together could renew their baptismal promises while holding the lit candles from their baptisms (or other candles). The family could also enjoy a "birthday cake" of some kind, since through baptism, we are reborn as children of God.

Candlemas Day, the Feast of the Presentation, February 2

In Eastern European countries like Poland, the feast of the Presentation of the Lord marks the end of the Christmas season—forty days after the celebration of the birth of our Lord. For this reason, Pope St. John Paul II had the crèche kept in St. Peter's Square through this day, a tradition that continues to this day. (I keep my parish church decorated and my rectory Christmas tree—albeit an artificial one—decorated through this day.)

Candlemas Day is another name for the feast of the Presentation of the Lord. Forty days after his birth, Mary and Joseph brought Jesus to the Temple for the rites of purification and dedication as prescribed by the Torah. According to the book of Leviticus (12:1–4), when a woman bore a male child, she was considered "unclean" for seven days. On the eighth day, the boy was circumcised. The mother continued to stay at home for thirty-three days for her blood to be purified. After the forty days, the mother and the father came to the Temple for the rite of purification, which included the offering of a sacrifice: a lamb for a holocaust (burnt offering) and a pigeon or turtledove for a sin offering, or for a poor couple who could not afford a lamb, two pigeons or two turtle-doves. Note that Joseph and Mary made the offering of the poor (see Lk 2:24).

Also, Joseph and Mary were obliged by the Torah to "redeem" their firstborn son: "The Lord spoke to Moses and said, 'Conse-crate to me every first-born that opens the womb among the Isra-elites, both of man and beast, for it belongs to me'" (Ex 13:1). The price for such a redemption was five shekels, which the par-ents paid to the priest. This "redemption" was a kind of payment for the Passover sacrifice, by which the Jews had been freed from slavery.

However, St. Luke in the Gospel does not mention this redemp-tion, but rather the presentation of our Lord, that time when, according to the law of Moses, every first-born male should be "consecrated to the Lord'" (Lk 2:22–23). So, then, the focus is on Jesus's consecration to God. The verb "to present" (parista-nai) also means to "offer," which evokes Jesus being presented as the priest who will offer himself as the perfect sacrifice to free us from the slavery of sin, seal the new and eternal covenant with his blood, and open the gates to the true Promised Land of heaven.

Simeon, a just and pious man who awaited the Messiah and looked for the consolation of Israel, was inspired to come to the Temple. He held baby Jesus in his arms and blessed God, saying, "Now, Master, you may let your servant go in peace, according to your word, for my eyes have seen your salvation, which you prepared in sight of all the peoples, a light for revelation to the Gentiles, and glory for your people Israel" (Lk 2:29–32). Simeon, thereby, announced that the Messiah has come to save not just the Jew but also the Gentile; not just the righteous but also the sinner.

He then blessed the Holy Family and said in turn to Mary: "Behold, this child is destined [to be] the fall and rise of many in Israel, and to be a sign that will be contradicted (and you yourself a sword will pierce)" (Lk 2:34–35).

The Presentation is a proclamation of Christ—Messiah and Priest, Lord and Savior. He is the light who came into this world to dispel sin and darkness. For this reason, candles traditionally have been blessed at Mass this day which will be used throughout the year, hence coining the term "Candlemas."

As we consider the feast of the Presentation, we remember that at our parents presented us at church for our baptism. We were dedicated to God and given the name "Christian." We too received a lit candle from the paschal candle, at which the priest said, "You have been enlightened by Christ. Walk always as a child of the light and keep the flame of faith alive in your heart. When the Lord comes, may you go out to meet him with all the saints in the heavenly kingdom" (*Rite of Christian Initiation of Adults*). Therefore, as a light, each of us must bear witness to our Lord. We must be the beacon that guides others to Christ. Also, we must realize that we too will be "a sign that will be opposed," especially on issues of the sanctity of human life, marriage, and the family. Nevertheless, as St. Teresa of Calcutta said, "Better to light a candle than curse the darkness."

Here is another interesting tidbit: Candlemas Day also was important in the lives of farmers. An old English song went as follows:

> If Candlemas be fair and bright,
> Come Winter, have another flight.
> If Candlemas brings clouds and rain,
> Go, Winter, and come not again.

If the bright sun "overshadows" the brightness of Candlemas Day, there will be more winter. However, if the light of Candlemas Day radiates through the gloom and darkness of the day, the end of winter is near. Keep in mind, in America, the Protestants decided we should replace Catholic Candlemas Day with a Groundhog Day.

Postscript

I hope and pray that you have found this collection of traditions, stories, meditations, and spiritual activities useful for your Christmas preparation and celebration. Moreover, I hope you, dear readers, appreciate more and more the beauty of our Catholic faith. The goal now is to put Christ back into our Christmas celebration and make it a celebration of his *presence*, not simply of *presents*. May the promise of Scrooge in *A Christmas Carol* be ours: "I will honor Christmas in my heart, and try to keep it all the year." May the Lord's blessings descend upon you and remain with you and your loved ones this Christmas.

About the Author

Father William P. Saunders was born on March 9, 1957 in Washington, D.C. to Dr. Joseph F. and Pauline C. Saunders. In 1959, his family moved to Springfield, Virginia where he was raised. He has one older brother, Joseph F. Saunders, Jr.

After graduating from West Springfield High School as the class valedictorian in 1975, he attended the College of William and Mary, Williamsburg, Virginia. He graduated in 1979 with a Bachelor of Business Administration degree in Accounting and with membership in Beta Gamma Sigma Honor Society.

During the summer after college graduation, Father Saunders focused on the vocation to the priesthood, with which he had been wrestling since college. He applied to the Diocese of Arlington, Virginia for admission into the seminary, and was assigned to St. Charles Borromeo Seminary, Philadelphia, Pennsylvania. In 1984, Father Saunders graduated from St. Charles Seminary with a Master of Arts in Sacred Theology, *Summa cum laude*, and was ordained to the Holy Priesthood on May 12.

As a priest, Father Saunders has served as the Assistant Pastor at St. Mary Catholic Church in Alexandria, VA (1984–1988), the Campus Chaplain and Adjunct Professor of Theology for Marymount University, Arlington, VA (1988–1993), the Assistant Pastor (1993–95) and subsequently the Pastor (1995–2000) at Queen of Apostles Catholic Church in Alexandria, Virginia. In the summer of 2000, he was assigned as the founding pastor of Our Lady of Hope Catholic Church in Potomac Falls, Virginia, where he continues to serve.

During this time, Father Saunders pursued studies at Catholic University, receiving a Doctor of Philosophy in Education Administration in 1992.

He was appointed as President of the Notre Dame Institute for Catechetics in 1992, a graduate school offering a Master of Arts in Catechetics, Sacred Scripture, and Spirituality. On February 1, 1997, the Notre Dame Institute officially merged with Christendom College, Front Royal, Virginia, becoming the Notre Dame Graduate School. At that time, Father Saunders was appointed Dean of the Graduate School.

From 1993 to 2006, Father Saunders wrote a weekly column entitled "Straight Answers" for the *Arlington Catholic Herald*, the diocesan newspaper. In 1998, he published a book by the same title, *Straight Answers*, and in 2003, a second volume, *Straight Answers II*. To mark the dedication of Our Lady of Hope Church and School, he published *A Labor of Love* in 2008. He continues to write periodically for the *Arlington Catholic Herald* and other publications.

Bibliography

The information in this book represents my thirty-four years of preaching and teaching. Some of the most prominent sources include the following:

Butler's Lives of the Saints. Notre Dame, IN: Christian Classics, 1956.

Carroll, Warren H. *Our Lady of Guadalupe and the Conquest of Darkness*. Front Royal, VA: Christendom Press, 1983.

Cirlot, J. E. *A Dictionary of Symbols*. New York: Philosophical Library, 1962.

Customs and Traditions of the Catholic Family. Long Prairie, MN: The Neumann Press, 1994.

Fisher, Celia. *Flowers and Fruit*. London: The National Gallery, 1998.

Gall, Dom Roberrt Le Gall, Abbot of Kergonan. *Symbols of Catholicism*. New York: Assouline, 1996.

Klein, Peter. *The Catholic Source Book*. Orlando, FL: Brown-ROA, 2000.

Matford, J. C. J. *Dictionary of Christian Lore and Legend*. London: Thames and Hudson Ltd., 1983.

Merck, Timothy & Beth. *Christmas Ornament Legends: The Definitive Collection of Stories, Traditions, and Folklore*. Spokane, WA: Merck Family's Old World Christmas, 2001.

Ornament Legends, Symbols, and Traditions. Frankenmuth, MI: Bronner's CHRISTmas Wonderland, 2004.

Ratzinger, Joseph (Pope Benedict XVI). *The Blessing of Christmas*. San Francisco, CA: Ignatius Press, 2005

Ratzinger, Joseph (Pope Benedict XVI). *Jesus of Nazareth: The Infancy Narratives*. New York: Image Books, 2012.

Sheen, Fulton J. *The World's First Love*. New York: McGraw-Hill Book Company, Inc., 1952.

Van Dyke, Henry. "The Oak of Geismar." *The Christmas Story Book*. Long Prairie, MN: The Neumann Press, nd.

Weiser, Francis X. *Religious Customs in the Family*. Rockford, IL: TAN Books and Publishers, Inc., 1956.

Image Credits

p. vi: *The Adoration of the Magi* (detail), 1423 (tempera on wood) / Gentile da Fabriano. Public domain via Wikimedia Commons.
p. viii: *Christmas Gifts Under the Tree* / Mikhail_Kayl / Shutterstock.
p. 3: *Nativity Scene* (photo) / Alexander Hoffman / Shutterstock.
p. 4–5: *Advent Candles* (photo) / Godong/UIG / Bridgeman Images.
p. 6: *The Annunciation*, D. Ferrari, Restored Traditions.
p. 8: *The Visitation*, Raphael (Raffaello Sanzio of Urbino) (1483-1520) / Prado, Madrid, Spain / Bridgeman Images.
p. 10: *The Archangel Gabriel*, c. 1430 (tempera on panel), Masolino da Panicale, Tommaso (1383-c.1447) / National Gallery of Art, Washington DC, USA / Bridgeman Images.
p. 13: *Advent Candles* (photo) / Godong/UIG / Bridgeman Images.
p. 20: *St. Nicholas of Bari*, 1539 (oil on canvas), Moretto da Brescia. Public domain via Wikimedia Commons.
p. 23: *Saint Nicholas*, 1745-1750 (oil on canvas), Francesco Guardi. Public domain via Wikimedia Commons.
p. 27: *St. Nicholas in the Act of Cutting Down a Tree Worshiped by Heathens*, 17th century (oil on panel), Leonardo Corona. Public domain via Wikimedia Commons.
p. 28: *The Immaculate Conception*, 1767-1768 (oil on canvas), Giovanni Battista Tiepolo. Public domain via Wikimedia Commons.
p. 35: *La Inmaculada Concepción*, 18th century (oil on canvas), Anton Raphael Mengs. Public domain via Wikimedia Commons.
p. 36: *Vigin of Guadalupe*, 1779 (oil on copper panel). Public domain via Wikimedia Commons.
p. 39: *Fiel retrato do venerável Juan Diego*, 1752, Miguel Cabrera. Public domain via Wikimedia Commons.
p. 45: *Virgin of Guadalupe statue on the facade of the Temple of the Congregation in Queretaro, Mexico. Consecrated in 1680* (photo) / Bryan Busovicki / Shutterstock.
p. 49: *St. Lucy*, 1535–1540 (oil on wood), Benvenuto Tisi. Public domain via Wikimedia Commons.
p. 50: *Lucia in Vaxholm, Stockholm*, Sweden 2017 (photo), Bengt Nyman. Public domain via Wikimedia Commons.
p. 54: *Saint Joseph Carpenter*, 1640s (oil on canvas), Georges de La Tour. Public domain via Wikimedia Commons.
p. 57: *The Dream of St. Joseph*, 1773–1774 (oil on oak), Anton Raphael Mengs. Public domain via Wikimedia Commons.
p. 59: *St. Joseph Carrying the Infant Jesus*, 1665 (oil on canvas), Letellier, Pierre (1614-76) / Musee des Beaux-Arts, Rouen, France / Bridgeman Images.
p. 66: *The Nativity with the Prophet Isaiah*, 1308–1311 (tempera on panel), Duccio di Buonisegna. Public domain via Wikimedia Commons.
p. 71: *The Concert of Angels*, 1534-36 (fresco) (detail) (see 175762), Ferrari, Gaudenzio (1474/80-1546) / Sanctuary of Santa Maria delle Grazie, Saronno, Italy / Bridgeman Images.

p. 74–75: *Christmas Celebration* (photo) / Godong/UIG / Bridgeman Images

p. 76: *A Partridge in a Pear Tree* / Eireann / Shutterstock.

p. 82: *Christmas Tree with Presents* / K2 PhotoStudio / Shutterstock.

p. 87: *Saint Boniface*, Godfrey, Michael (20th century) / Private Collection / © Look and Learn / Bridgeman Images.

p. 89: *Silent Night*, 1891 (oil on canvas), Johansen, Viggo (1851-1935) / Hirschsprung-ske Samling, Copenhagen, Denmark / Bridgeman Images.

p. 92: AB/130 *A Christmas Arrangement*, Williams, Albert (1922-2010) / Private Collection / Bridgeman Images.

p. 96: *Watercolor with Holly Leaves, Berries and Spruce Branches,* Calesh / Shutterstock.

p. 101: *St. Francis of Assisi Preparing the Christmas Crib at Grecchio,* 1296-97 (fresco), Giotto di Bondone (c.1266-1337) / San Francesco, Upper Church, Assisi, Italy / Bridgeman Images.

p. 104: *Christ's Nativity*, Mi. Ti. / Shutterstock.

p. 108: *Christmas Candle in Window*, tab62 / Shutterstock.

p. 114: *100th Jubilee of First Performance of Silent Night* / Lebrecht Music Arts / Bridgeman Images.

p. 117: *A Child Singing a Carol*, Jacob_09 / Shutterstock.

p. 121: *Nativity* (oil on canvas), Champaigne, Philippe de (1602-74) / Musee des Beaux-Arts, Lille, France / Bridgeman Images.

p. 124: *The Holy Family*, J. Palinka / Restored Traditions.

p. 129: *The Christmas Tree*, 1911 (oil on canvas), Tayler, Albert Chevallier (1862-1925) / Private Collection / Bridgeman Images.

p. 135: *Madonna and Child*, Sassoferrato, Il (Giovanni Battista Salvi) (1609-85) / Kunsthistorisches Museum, Vienna, Austria / Bridgeman Images.

p. 138: *High Altar Depicting Yahweh*, 2C2C / Shutterstock.

p. 142: *XP, Crismon, Monogram* (photo) / Godong/UIG / Bridgeman Images.

p. 144: *Three Wise Men* (gouache on paper), Coller, Henry (1886-1958) / Private Collection / © Look and Learn / Bridgeman Images.

p. 149: *Adoration of the Magi*, C. Dolci / Restored Traditions.

p. 157: *The Adoration of the Magi*, 1904 (tapestry), Edward Burne-Jones. Public domain via Wikimedia Commons.

p. 158: *The Baptism of Christ*, 1622–1623 (oil on canvas), Guido Reni. Public domain via Wikimedia Commons.

p. 164: *Presentation of Jesus in the Temple*, 1510 (panel), Carpaccio, Vittore (c.1460/5-1523/6) / Gallerie dell'Accademia, Venice, Italy / Mondadori Portfolio/Electa/Osvaldo Böhm / Bridgeman Images.

p. 170: *Christmas at the Vatican*, Antony McAuley / Shutterstock.

p. 176: *Nativity*, C. Coypel / Restored Traditions.